Georgetown Journal
of International Affairs

Forum: A Post-Snowden Cyberspace

Safety&Security

T0346399

Georgetown Journal

of International Affairs

INTERNATIONAL ENGAGEMENT ON CYBER IV

MANAGING EDITOR AZHAR UNWALA

EXECUTIVE DIRECTOR LUCAS CHAN

EDITORIAL STAFF

ASSOCIATE EDITORS ZACH BURDETTE, SHABAB HUSSAIN, BRANDON KELLEY, CHRISTOPHER KNOX, HALEY LEPP, RINA LI, ANDREW McCOY, DEBORAH OU-YANG, ILYANA OVSHIEVA, LETITIA WU

DESIGN STAFF

DESIGN DIRECTORS YULI LIN, MALLIKA SEN
DESIGN ASSISTANT ALLESANDRA TYLER

ADVISORY BOARD DAVID ABSHIRE, SUSAN BENNETT, HIS MAJESTY KING FELIPE IV, CARA DIMASSA, ROBERT L. GALLUCCI, MICHAEL MAZARR, JENNIFER WARD, FAREED ZAKARIA

UNIVERSITY COUNCIL JEFFREY ANDERSON (CHAIR), ANTHONY CLARK AREND, MARC BUSCH, MATTHEW CARNES, VICTOR CHA, RAJ DESAI, CHARLES DOLGAS, JOHN ESPOSITO, MARK GIORDANO, MITCH KANEDA, CHRISTINE KIM, CHARLES KING, MARK LAGON, ERIC LANGENBACHER, JOANNA LEWIS, CATHERINE LOTRIONTE, KATHERINE MARSHALL, SUSAN MARTIN, KATHLEEN McNAMARA, JOHN McNEIL, JAMES MILLWARD, DANIEL NEXON, DAVID PAINTER, STEVEN RADELET, GEORGE SHAMBAUGH, ELIZABETH STANLEY, SCOTT, TAYLOR, CHARLES WEISS, JENNIFER WINDSOR

THANKS

IN CONCLUDING THIS ISSUE, I AM EXTREMELY GRATEFUL TO OUR CONTRIBUTORS AS WELL AS OUR DEDICATED STAFF FOR THEIR TIRELESS WORK. I WOULD ALSO LIKE TO THANK DR. CATHERINE LOTRIONTE AND ALLYSON GOODWIN FOR THEIR EXPERTISE, UNWAVERING COMMITMENT, AND STEADFAST ADVICE. I HOPE YOU WILL ENJOY THIS *CYBER* ISSUE OF THE *GEORGETOWN JOURNAL OF INTERNATIONAL AFFAIRS*.

—AZHAR UNWALA

The
Georgetown Journal of International Affairs
would like to thank the following sponsors

To become a sponsor, contact:
Victoria Moroney
Edmund A. Walsh School of Foreign Service, Georgetown University
ICC 301, 3700 O Street, N.W., Washington, DC 20057
Telephone (847) 691-0030
gjia@georgetown.edu

Notice to Contributors

Articles submitted to the *Georgetown Journal of International Affairs* must be original, must not draw substantially from articles previously published by the author, and must not be simultaneously submitted to any other publication. Articles should be around 3,000 words in length. Manuscripts must be typewritten and double-spaced in Microsoft™ Word® format, with margins of at least one inch. Authors should follow the *Chicago Manual of Style, 15th ed.* Articles may be submitted by e-mail (gjia@georgetown.edu). Full names of authors, a two-sentence biography, and contact information including addresses with zip codes, telephone numbers, facsimile numbers, and e-mail addresses must accompany each submission. The *Georgetown Journal of International Affairs* will consider all manuscripts submitted, but assumes no obligation regarding publication. All material submitted is returnable at the discretion of the *Georgetown Journal of International Affairs*.

The *Georgetown Journal of International Affairs* (ISSN 1526-0054; ISBN 978-1-62616-216-7) is published twice yearly by Georgetown University Press for the Edmund A. Walsh School of Foreign Service, Georgetown University. Subscription rates: Domestic: $16.00; foreign: $24.00; Canada: $18.00; institutions: $40.00.

Editorial Offices

Georgetown Journal of International Affairs
Edmund A. Walsh School of Foreign Service
Georgetown University
301 Intercultural Center
3700 O Street, NW
Washington, DC 20057
gjia@georgetown.edu

Subscriptions

Georgetown Journal of International Affairs
Subscriptions
c/o Johns Hopkins University Press
Journals Publishing Division
P.O. Box 19966
Baltimore, MD 21211-0966
Phone: 1-800-548-1784 or 410-516-6987
Fax: 410-516-3866
www.press.georgetown.edu

Publisher

Georgetown University Press
3240 Prospect Street, NW
Suite 250
Washington, DC 2007
www.press.georgetown.edu
gupress@georgetown.edu

Backlist, Single-Copy, and Bulk Sales

Georgetown University Press
c/o Hopkins Fulfillment Service
P.O. Box 50370
Baltimore, MD 21211-4370
Phone: 1-800-537-5487 or
410-516-6998
www.press.georgetown.edu

Forum

GEORGETOWN JOURNAL OF INTERNATIONAL AFFAIRS

A Post–Snowden Cyberspace

The study and practice of cybersecurity is inherently interdisciplinary, implicating disparate bodies of technical, legal and policy expertise. The questions involved in guarding against cyberthreats are exceptionally diverse because the threats in cyberspace themselves take on so many forms, ranging from attacks on critical infrastructure perpetrated by governments and non-state actors, theft of trade secrets by government entities or their proxies, state espionage, theft by corporate insiders or government employees, cybercrime by organized criminal groups and DDOS attacks by hacktivists. These threats target different vulnerabilities and call for a comprehensive strategy for countering them. Debates continue to arise over how the Internet will be governed in order to maintain its interoperability and stability with access to all. And tensions rise between states over sovereign uses of intelligence collection through the Internet.

At the same time, uncertainty about the magnitude of the threats and the rights and obligations of private and public actors has clouded the path to developing a most effective technological, policy and legal approach for governing cyberspace. Future generations of computer security experts, lawyers and policymakers will be called upon to address cybersecurity challenges and therefore need to become more conversant in the nuances of the technical, policy and legal issues. In that vein, in the spring of each year, under the auspices of the CyberProject, Georgetown University convenes for a one-day international conference, leading international experts in these areas to address the cutting-edge issues of cybersecurity.

In partnership with the *Georgetown Journal of International Affairs*, we work to assemble a number of articles from leading scholars and practitioners to publish in the annual *International Engagement on Cyber* series to broaden the dialogue and help develop the field. Many of the authors in the current and past issues have been speakers at the international conference and we hope that new authors will consider joining us for the annual conference. As with the conference, the series aims to inform current and future academics, practitioners and students about the wide range of issues they will confront in their work about cybersecurity and assist them in refining the expertise necessary to address the toughest of the challenges ahead.

This fourth edition of our annual *International Engagement in Cyber* series begins with a group of articles in the Forum section entitled "A Post-Snowden Cyberspace," describing how the Snowden revelations directly or indirectly changed the way the global community understands cybersecurity and cyber law. David Weinstein explains how Snowden affected U.S. credibility in cyberspace, while Franz-Stefan Gady compares U.S. and EU data privacy laws in a post-Snowden political climate. Given what has come to light about NSA surveillance, Anja Mihr proposes that global human rights law ought to be applied in the cyber domain. According to Milton Mueller, the Snowden revelations, in exposing U.S. cyber dominance, made it politically feasible for the transition of the IANA functions away from the Commerce Department, while Sandro Gaycken discusses how Snowden's actions resulted in a greater awareness about IT security vulnerabilities and the need for better defenses.

To kick off the second section of the issue entitled "Safety & Security," co-authors Melissa Hathaway and John Stewart argue that to make a difference in cybersecurity at scale, four actions are necessary from two points of view: one towards technology and practice and another towards policy and law. The actions address the need for connected devices to have minimum standards and for security practitioners to return to basic fundamentals of network security while aiming to change market behavior and require organizational and executive accountability for cybersecurity. In a compelling argument, the authors show a need to anticipate tomorrow's demands for network capacity, new applications and meeting the needs of an expanding base of users with security today. Continuing to focus on the role of the private sector, author Amitai Etzioni argues that companies must increase their level of cybersecurity given that much of U.S. critical infrastructure depends on the private sector for its security. Wrapping up this discussion, authors Lawrence Gordon, Martin Loeb and William Lucyshyn tackle the systemic problem of under-investment in cybersecurity by private firms.

Focusing on a country-specific approach to cybersecurity, Yoko Nitta provides a view into how Japan's cyber-security strategy has developed along with its approach to international collaboration. In our final section,

"Military Matters," five authors analyze how cyber technology will matter in conflict. Jarno Limnell develops a case for keeping the command and control of cyber weapons at the highest level of government while Maj. Gen. Charles J Dunlap, Jr describes how the development of new technologies along with "Big Data" analytical methodologies will provide new opportunities for warfighters and long-term implications for "cyber-war." Richard Andres argues that the general literature on cyber strategy is wrong in that states indeed can use cyber weapons as tools for bargaining and diplomacy. He illustrates the three main ways states are using offensive weapons to achieve political objectives by force and fraud and diplomatic efforts to prevent retaliation and escalation. Ben Buchanan takes on the notion of cyber-deterrence, arguing that not one form of deterrence but a "mosaic" response of multiple kinds of deterrence could achieve overall deterrence in cyberspace. Greg Austin concludes the issue with an article that offers insight into the strategic imbal-ance between the U.S. and China when it comes to cyber military power and its future implications for "mutual" security in cyberspace.

We at the CyberProject and the *Georgetown Journal of International Affairs* have been very fortunate to work with such experts on this issue and want to thank the authors for their diligence in bringing this issue to fruition and expanding the debate to the broader public. We know that the insights and scholarship of these articles will help develop the field of cybersecurity and improve the level of discussion. We thank you for your continued support in our efforts at Georgetown University to contribute to the discipline.

Dr. Catherine Lotrionte

DIRECTOR, CYBERPROJECT
SCHOOL OF FOREIGN SERVICE
GEORGETOWN UNIVERSITY
LOTRIONC@GEORGETOWN.EDU

Snowden and U.S. Cyber Power

Dave Weinstein

In June 2013, Edward Snowden, a twenty-nine-year-old former National Security Agency (NSA) contractor without a college diploma, executed the single largest leak of classified intelligence in modern American history. He did so with the cooperation of select journalists, media outlets, and a coalition of other supporters. Just four days after transferring the encrypted classified data to two journalists in Hong Kong, Snowden revealed his identity and motivations in a lengthy interview that quickly proliferated across the Internet.

The merits of Snowden's actions remain vigorously contested in the public sphere. On one side, civil libertarians praise Snowden for shedding light on what they consider a monumental invasion of privacy and violation of civil liberties. Alternatively, others scorn the Moscow-based fugitive for committing grave damage to U.S. national security interests and its reputation abroad. This text scrutinizes the latter position but measures "grave damage" in the context of U.S. cyber power and not the often-debated realm of American intelligence or diplomacy. It does not aim to diminish Snowden's impact on U.S. intelligence and foreign policy, but rather expand the dialogue to broader and perhaps less obvious consequences.

Dave Weinstein is a cyber-security consultant and affiliated with the Council on Foreign Relations' Program on Digital and Cyberspace Policy. For three years he was a Strategic Operations Planner at U.S. Cyber Command.

Indeed, there is little disagreement that Snowden's bulk release of classified documents to the press impaired the United States' intelligence apparatus. In a humble public admission, the Director of National Intelligence

ed fashion. In recent years, however, new military capabilities have emerged outside of the traditional domains of kinetic warfare. These capabilities exist in cyberspace and although relative cyber power is more difficult to quan-

Cyberspace's low barriers to entry complicate traditional balance of power models by introducing heretofore absent actors into the arena, often eroding otherwise powerful states' power.

James Clapper offered testimony before the Senate Intelligence Committee that Snowden caused "profound damage" to America's collection posture.[1] The leaked documents included detailed information on American signals intelligence (SIGINT) sources and methods, a highly coveted treasure for any adversary of the United States. But compromised intelligence techniques and a diminished suite of tools offer a tactical perspective of Snowden's impact. Time will ultimately mitigate the operational setbacks promulgated by the leaks, but the strategic perspective reveals Snowden's impact on the United States' relative cyber power. The following introduces the elements of cyber power and then assesses Snowden's revelations relative to each element.

Elements of Cyber Power. To date, most international relations theorists calculate power by interpreting states' relative military capabilities in sea, air, and on land. At least among realists, a state's power is often judged by its ability to project force in each domain, both independently and in an integrat-

tify than sea, air, or land power, it is nonetheless pivotal in today's digital age. The addition of cyberspace to the global power dynamic is problematic for most conventional theorists, namely because its attributes differ so greatly from other domains. In particular, there are three characteristics of cyberspace that differentiate cyber power from kinetic power.

First, cyberspace has extremely low barriers to entry. Not only are cyber capabilities much less expensive than kinetic capabilities, but they are also generally accessible to a broader pool of state and non-state actors. For example, a report released by Arbor Security Engineering & Response Team, or SERT, in February 2012 compiled data on commercially available distributed denial of service (DDoS) attack tools. One tool, known as Darkness X, is regularly advertised on popular hacker forums and sells for between $499 and $999 depending on the specifications.[2] Similarly, the human capital necessary to develop and maintain cyber power is far less than, for example, the human capital necessary to develop and maintain air power. A single person is capable of reverse engineering, developing, and testing malware payloads whereas the development and testing cycles of a missile requires the participation of multidisciplinary stakeholders with expertise in aerodynamics, propulsion, and physics. Ultimately, cyberspace's low barriers to entry complicate traditional balance of power models by introducing heretofore absent actors into the arena, often eroding otherwise powerful states' power.

Second, cyberspace offers the comfort of limited attribution for its actors. This characteristic yields two complications. First, the anonymity of cyberspace hinders deterrence. For example, the Cold War tactics of mutually assured destruction are not applicable to cyberspace if states' operations are sufficiently obfuscated. Furthermore, and closely related, cyberspace's inherent anonymity often allows actors to evade any perception of possessing power beyond kinetic force. This exemption heightens the prospect for miscalculation between states when relative power assessments only consider sea, air, and land forces. Russia's 2008 ground invasion of Georgia illustrates how non-kinetic capabilities can significantly supplement a state's relative power and therefore deserve consideration commensurate with kinetic capabilities.

And the third characteristic of cyberspace is its offensive dominant nature. Based on a rational cost-benefit calculation, attackers have little incentive not to seize the initiative and assume an offensive posture in cyberspace. As with limited attribution, the attacker's offensive advantage also compli-cates deterrence strategies. Moreover, in other domains states seek to preserve the balance of power by constructing defensive capabilities to balance against offensive build-ups. The security dilemma ensues when defensive balancing is perceived to threaten the balanced state, thereby resulting in a vicious cycle of militarization. But in cyberspace, the security dilemma does not apply. No defensive build-up is capable of threatening the offensive actor because, by virtue of the domain's aforementioned characteristics, the attacker is inherently advantaged. Instead, this persistent vulnerability for the defender yields the *vulnerability* dilemma, a state in which an actor's protection from cyber threats depends solely on its ability to influence the will of the threatening actor.

Lowering the Barriers to Entry.

Having established some key elements of cyber power, it is important to scrutinize Snowden's actions in this context. Snowden's damage to the United States was not only revealing sources and methods or compromising tools, but also diminishing America's cyber power in an increasingly competitive pool of actors.

First, Snowden's actions succeeded in lowering cyberspace's already low barriers to entry. By revealing highly sensitive cyber tradecraft, Snowden exposed an even greater pool of state and non-state actors to some of America's most sophisticated tools and techniques, thereby decreasing the United States' relative cyber power. Despite the domain's low barriers to entry, some elements of cyber power are not easily acquired and retained. It is these elements that states seek to contain from public disclosure in order to elevate the barriers to entry for other actors. Nevertheless, the leaks provided increased opportunities for America's adversarial cyber actors to acquire such elements that would otherwise exist beyond their reach.

For relatively advanced cyber powers such as the United States, this characteristic of cyberspace benefits its state and non-state adversaries more than itself because it grants them asymmetric capabilities to mitigate America's conventional superiority. As cyberspace's barriers to entry lower, America's relative cyber power decreases. In this respect, Snowden's leaks undoubtedly contributed to narrowing the cyber power gap between the United States and other notable players in the virtual arena.

Removing Anonymity and Mitigating the Offensive Advantage.
Second, Snowden's actions succeeded in removing the anonymity associated with American cyber power. States and non-states derive significant cyber power from obfuscating their operations because it complicates cyber defense and deterrence strategies, but also yields an unparalleled freedom of maneuver compared to other domains. Furthermore, the United States' ability to attribute other states' operations in cyberspace is equally critical to amassing cyber power. In this respect, Snowden's actions compromised not only the United States' anonymity in cyberspace, but also, and perhaps more importantly, its ability to attribute other states' cyberspace operations for the purpose of cyber defense and ultimately, deterrence.

Closely related is the issue of offensive dominance. Cyberspace inherently advantages the attacker provided the attacker sufficiently obfuscates its operations. The Snowden leaks, however, compromised America's operational anonymity in cyberspace. The offensive advantage is manifested not only in the form of operational anonymity, but also political immunity. In this respect, Snowden's actions largely removed the United States' ability to plausibly deny its cyber power, a critical tool relied upon by most cyber powers in today's virtual geopolitical landscape.

Enabling Cyber Power.
In addition to hindering America intelligence and diplomatic efforts, revealing sensitive sources and methods also damages U.S. cyber power. Intelligence, although it is not necessarily an element of cyber power, is indeed a key enabler of it. And in today's digital word, SIGINT, the focus of Snowden's revelations, is particularly relevant.

There is little empirical evidence to support the notion that the United States is the world's most advanced practitioner of SIGINT. However, if Snowden's focus on the breadth and scope of what he termed America's "surveillance state" is any indication of American SIGINT prowess, then the United States is certainly a top player in the field. Furthermore, the United States' history of pioneering SIGINT capabilities dates back to World War II when its cryptologic advantages over both Japan and Nazi Germany earned strategic victories for the U.S. and Allied forces. Just as it served as a competitive advantage during the advent of analog communications, the proliferation of hyper-connected networks during the digital age renders it an even stronger enabler of national power.

Snowden's revelations, therefore, have succeeded in not only compromising America's near-term technical capabilities, but more importantly, threatening its long-term preeminence in the field. The leaks offer a wealth of

to levels of international scrutiny that were previously reserved for its steepest competitors in the digital domain.

Diminished Credibility. If intelligence plays a role in enabling cyber power, then credibility aids in maintaining it. Prior to Snowden's leaks, the United States derived signifi-

The Snowden leaks left American credibility severely tattered at precisely the same time that America's adversaries were in jeopardy of commanding almost no international credibility on cyberspace policy whatsoever.

knowledge to adversarial states seeking to better enable their cyber power relative to the United States. The documents revealed by various media outlets will undoubtedly aid other states in advancing their technical intelligence and counter-intelligence techniques and ultimately, improving their absolute cyber power.

In addition, Snowden's actions prompted a domestic and international debate on surveillance that, regardless of merit, disadvantages the United States relative to its otherwise less capable adversaries. The biggest winners (incidentally also the two countries to which Snowden fled following the initial leaks) are China and Russia, states that have historically received significant international criticism for surveillance practices but also maintain a highly competitive relationship with the United States on matters of technical espionage. The Snowden leaks, however, have subjected the United States

cant credibility on cyber issues from its legitimacy on a range of policies and practices. Moreover, it possessed a highly regarded reputation for leadership on Internet governance topics and, mainly due to the general illegitimate standing of other cyber powers, the United States enjoyed widespread support to pursue its policy objectives in international forums. But in the wake of Snowden's revelations, the United States' international credibility on these issues plummeted. Whether or not this rapid downward trajectory was warranted is another debate altogether (and beyond the scope of this text). Nevertheless, fueled by intense media obsession, the United States' credibility on cyberspace policy transformed from a position of strength to one of weakness almost overnight. Friendly states, facing domestic political opposition, distanced themselves from the U.S. on cyberspace policy and, at times even participated in the public condemnation. Adversarial states, meanwhile, swiftly joined the chorus of criticism seeking to harm America's credibility and, in turn, enhance their cyber power vis-à-vis the United States. In the court of public opinion, the Snowden leaks left American credibility severely tattered at precisely the same time that America's adversaries were in jeopardy of commanding almost no international credibility on cyberspace policy whatsoever. In this respect, the timely leaks provided a welcomed distraction for states typically faced with domestic surveillance criticisms.

Conclusion and Recommendations.
If Snowden's leaks revealed anything, they revealed the extent of American cyber power to the world. In doing so, though, the leaks threatened the very elements from which the United States derives this power. In particular, Snowden's actions succeeded in lowering cyberspace's already low barriers to

Snowden's actions beyond the context of just intelligence and diplomatic setbacks. The damage to the United States' intelligence posture and its diplomatic standing on Internet governance and surveillance issues is not insignificant; but given the growing importance of cyberspace as a venue for military and geopolitical interaction, perhaps the even more damaging development relates to Snowden's long-term threat to U.S. cyber power. In an environment as competitive as cyberspace, the United States must take three swifts steps to mitigate this threat.

First, policymakers must take steps to preserve America's operational anonymity in cyberspace while maintaining transparency on matters of cyberspace policy. The former will help America recover its cyber power relative to other actors that enjoy high levels of obfuscation in cyberspace and the latter will help the United States rebuild its credibility among domestic and inter-

American cyber operations deserve anonymity but, in the post-Snowden era, the policies that govern them warrant more public scrutiny.

entry, decreasing America's anonymity in cyberspace, and mitigating its inherent offensive advantage relative to other cyber actors. In addition to damaging the United States' longstanding credibility on cyberspace policy, Snowden's revelations compromised the very sources and methods that play a key role in enabling American cyber power.

It is important that policymakers, therefore, view the consequences of

national audiences. American cyber operations deserve anonymity but, in the post-Snowden era, the policies that govern them warrant more public scrutiny.

Second, policymakers must pursue more creative deterrence strategies to account for the United States' adversaries' growing relative offensive cyber advantage. Establishing clear and unambiguous thresholds for the use of force in cyberspace is a start, but American policymakers must supplement such thresholds with credible threats of retaliation not only in cyberspace, but also across all domains. Accruing international support for such policies would enhance the prospect for cyber deterrence regimes and revising the North Atlantic Treaty Organization's Article 5 to define armed attacks in cyberspace is a timely opportunity.

And third, the key to America's cyber power over the next decade will not be its offensive capabilities, but rather its ability to attribute beyond any reasonable doubt the source of malicious cyber behavior. If we have learned anything from Snowden's revelations, it is that states and their citizens are highly sympathetic to the victims of perceived cyber attack or espionage. For the United States to fully mitigate the impact of Snowden's leaks on its cyber power, it must reverse its perceived identity as a cyber aggressor and reveal in excruciating detail the degree to which it is a victim of cyber aggression. The United States' ability to demonstrate good stewardship of the global commons in contrast to attributable state and non-state aggression from its cyber adversaries will ultimately lead to America regaining its post atop the global cyber power index.

Disclaimer: The opinions expressed in in this article are solely those of the author.

NOTES

1 Worldwide Threat Assessment of the US Intelligence Community, United States Senate, 113ᵗʰ Congress, 2014, Statement of James R. Clapper, Director of National Intelligence, http://www.intelligence.senate.gov/140129/clapper.pdf.

2 Curt Wilson, "Attack of the Shuriken: Many Hands, Many Weapons," *DDoS and Security Report: The Arbor Networks Security Blog*, 7 February 2012, http://ddos.arbornetworks.com/2012/02/ddos-tools/.

3 Edward Snowden, interview by Glenn Greenwald, *The Guardian*, June 9, 2013.

EU/U.S. Approaches to Data Privacy and the "Brussels Effect"

A Comparative Analysis

Franz-Stefan Gady

The European Union and the United States differ in their respective approaches to data privacy. The former uses a strict top-down regulation system with heavy government involvement, whereas the latter relies on a "patchwork" approach— sectoral laws combined with industry self-regulation. This essay will compare EU and U.S. approaches to data privacy using Anu Bradford's "Brussels Effect" to explain the global ascendancy of the EU approach to data privacy protection. In addition, the paper will attempt to argue that Edward Snowden's revelations of a massive U.S.-sponsored surveillance program had the vicarious impact of strengthening proponents of stricter data protection laws within the EU, thereby amplifying the impact of the "Brussels Effect." For its conclusions, this article relies entirely on the reading of the letter of the law rather than the implementation and enforcement thereof. Such a comparative analysis, due to its complexity, is beyond the scope of this short analysis.

The U.S. Approach. Legal scholar Steven C. Bennett emphasizes that U.S. privacy law has "largely developed in a 'patchwork' with a 'reactive' array of state and federal statutes and common law doctrines."[1] In the United

Franz-Stefan Gady is a senior fellow at the East-West Institute, where he was a founding member of the Worldwide Cybersecurity Initiative. He was formerly an adjunct research assistant at the National Defense University's Institute for National Strategies Studies, and an analyst for the Project on National Security Reform. His research focuses on civil-military relations, revolution in military affairs, and cyber-diplomacy.

States, data privacy protection has its roots in the Fourth Amendment of the U.S. Constitution. Although it only deals with the protection of a citizen's home from unwarranted searches by the government, the amendment has been expanded to other contexts by case law that refined what constitutes a "search" based on technological developments over time.[2] For example, the United States Supreme Court recently ruled that the right to privacy as stated in the Fourth Amendment applies to cell phones and other digital devices used for communication, and that government authorities need a warrant to search such devices.[3] In the economic sphere, the Privacy Act of 1974—based on the concept of FIPPS (Fair Information Practice Principles)—is a general law protecting personal data of individuals in the United States.[4]

Protection against the unreasonable invasion of one's personal space by private parties was first discussed in the 1890 *Harvard Law Review* essay "The Right to Privacy," - co-authored by Samuel

dard common law defines torts as "civil wrongs recognized by law as grounds for a lawsuit".[7] Modern tort law recognizes four categories of invasion of privacy.[8] The United States also developed a number of statute-based sectoral privacy laws on the federal level as well as a general statute on consumer protection under the Federal Trade Commission Act (FTC), which protects personal data of U.S. consumers. The FTC, however, is not a national data protection agency in the proper sense, and there are various limits on the scope of the FTC's activities in the information privacy field. Furthermore, in February 2012, the White House announced a plan for the Consumer Privacy Bill of Rights, which has not made much progress in the last two years.[9] To date, the United States largely relies on industry self-regulation in the field of data privacy protection, which provides companies wide leeway in their usage of personal data to test new business practices, possibly resulting in privacy violations. This applies especially to enterprises in

The United States largely relies on industry self-regulation in the field of data privacy protection, which provides companies wide leeway in their usage of personal data to test new business practices, possibly resulting in privacy violations.

Warren and Louis Brandeis - which extolled "a right to be left alone."[5] At the state level, this right was developed by William Prosser and his concept of privacy tort, which according to Neil M. Richards, sits "at the heart of American understandings of privacy law."[6] Stan-

new business areas, as opposed to heavily regulated industries like telecommunications. As Paul M. Schwartz states, "The result of the sectoral approach in the United States makes newer technology companies a powerful voice in favor of the regulatory status quo."[10]

Furthermore, in the national security sphere, the Electronic Communications Privacy Act of 1986 —amended five times—regulates domestic surveillance for law enforcement, whereas the Foreign Intelligence Surveillance Act of 1978—amended multiple times over the last three decades—covers surveillance conducted to protect national security against foreign powers.[11, 12]

The EU Approach. The European Union is not a federal system; rather, it is based on the EU principle of "subsidiarity"—home state rule—with the consequence that data protection laws in the EU still vary widely among member states.[13] Like the U.S. Privacy Act of 1974, EU data privacy statutes are constructed around FIPPS. The 1890 essay "The Right to Privacy" also shaped the privacy debate in Europe with the German Federal Constitutional Court as recently as 1995 referencing *das Recht, allein gelassen zu werden* (the right to be left alone).[14]

The 1981 Council of Europe Convention on Personal Data Processing outlined general data protection commitments that "apply to all types of personal data processing by both government and private sectors."[15] The convention has been influential in developing national data protection laws across Europe. In addition, article 8 of the European Convention on Human Rights (ECHR) outlines respect for "his private and family life" (all 27 EU member states currently are contracting parties to the convention).[16]

Unlike the U.S. 1974 Privacy Act, the Charter of Fundamental Rights of the European Union, which came into force December 2009 following the Lisbon Treaty, requires data protection for everyone—not just EU citizens.[17] There is, however, a restriction on the right to privacy, and public authorities may interfere if it is "necessary in a democratic society in the interests of national security, public safety or the economic well-being of the country, for the prevention of disorder or crime, for the protection of health or morals, or for the protection of the rights and freedom of others."[18] Also, unlike in the United States where ownership belongs to the company or service that assembled the data, every individual has ownership of his data under European law.[19] The key EU legal document in this regard is the Data Protection Directive (Directive 95/46/EC), adopted in 1995, establishing common rules and processes for data privacy in the European Union.[20] EU directives are "harmonizing" instruments and not immediately binding. Member states of the European Union are required to pass national legislation that reflects their principles. The Data Protection Directive specifically outlines procedures for the collection, storage, use and disclosure of all personal data and places obligations on data controllers and confers rights on data subjects.[21] The EU and national governments influence data regulations through co-regulation, where a data protection authority (DPA), established in every member state, formulates binding corporate rules (BCRs) for companies. The Data Protection Directive has led to the establishment of omnibus privacy laws, which according to Paul M. Schwartz, "establish regulatory standards with a broad scope. Under the omnibus approach, sectoral laws are a backup used to increase the specificity of regulatory norms stemming from the initial statutory frameworks."[22]

In January 2012, the European Commission proposed a comprehensive reform of EU data protection rules with a new regulation to harmonize EU data privacy laws by establishing new uniform data protection requirements for all EU member states, including the "right to be forgotten."[23] According to the European Parliament, "The data protection reform package consists of two draft laws: a general regulation covering the bulk of personal data processing in the EU and a directive on processing data to prevent, investigate, detect or prosecute criminal offences or enforce criminal penalties."[24] This signals a shift from the previous status quo—unlike directives, EU regulations are binding on all member states.

A recent EU court ruling based on the principles underpinning the "right to be forgotten" already confirmed that individuals have the right under certain conditions to ask search engines to remove links with personal information about them.[25] In March 2014, the European Parliament voted overwhelmingly in favor of the new data regulations, yet internal political differences within the EU so far have hampered progress toward adoption of the new regulations by the European Council.[26, 27]

The Major Differences between the EU and US Approaches.

Generally speaking, it is evident that the European Union uses a strict regulation system that has broad effects on member states' approaches to privacy, whereas the United States relies on a "patchwork" approach—sectoral laws combined with industry self-regulation.

One of the major differences in this regard between the two systems is the regulation of cross-border data flows. As Julie Brill states, the United States "relied on holding those who transfer data accountable for its safe-keeping and self-regulatory codes of conduct to protect the privacy of personal information that flows across borders."[28] The EU's Data Privacy Directive is more restrictive. Article 25 of the directive allows the transfer of data to a third country only if the country "ensures an adequate level of protection."[29] The Article 29 Data Protection Working Group—comprised of members of representatives of the data protection authorities of each EU member state, the European Commission, and the European Data Protection Supervisor—states in an opinion from 1999, "the Working Party takes the view that the current patchwork of narrowly-focused sectoral laws and voluntary self-regulation cannot presently be relied upon to provide adequate protection in all cases for personal data transferred from the European Union."[30]

In 2001, the United States and the European Union agreed to a safe harbor approach, which stipulated that U.S. companies through self-certification at the corporate level could meet the "adequacy" requirements—basic privacy principles set forth in the EU Data Privacy Directive. It is important to note that the Safe Harbor agreement covers only personal data collected, controlled and used as a market good; whereas the EU data protection package covers both collection, control, and processing of personal data for economic (e.g. e-Commerce) and national security reasons. However, this important legal distinction becomes intangible when personal data is collected/given for one reason (joining a social network) and then used for another (fighting serious crime or tracking terrorists).[31]

In addition to the Safe Harbor agreement, Standard Contractual Clauses and Binding Corporate Rules were introduced for U.S. companies to meet the restrictive privacy standards of the EU.[32] The FTC is overseeing compliance with these standards. In 2011 and 2012 respectively, both Google and Facebook were found to be in violation of the agreement and accordingly fined.

The 2013 Snowden revelations led to a review of all the current EU-U.S. data-sharing agreements. In June 2014, the Irish High Court asked the European Court of Justice to review whether the Safe Harbor agreement is compatible with the EU Charter of Fundamental Rights after the revelation that Facebook shared EU citizens' data with the National Security Agency.[33] Regardless of the ruling, this announcement puts substantial pressure on U.S. companies to convince European officials that they are complying with strict European standards, or they risk being shut out of the EU's common market.

The Brussels Effect. In the article *The Brussels Effect*, Anu Bradford investigates "Europe's unilateral power to regulate global markets."[34] She particularly examines the globalization of standards and the way the EU successfully externalizes its regulations on other coun-

tries. According to Bradford, several conditions for this "unilateral regulatory globalization" must be met: a large domestic market, significant regulatory capacity, and the enforcement of strict rules over inelastic targets—all of which are met by the European Union.[35] Bradford states, "While the EU only regulates its internal market, multinational corporations often have an incentive to standardize their production globally and adhere to a single rule. This converts the EU rule into a global rule—the 'de facto Brussels Effect'." This is followed by a "de jure Brussels Effect" since companies have an "incentive to lobby their domestic governments to adopt these same standards in an effort to level the playing field against their domestic, non-export oriented competitors."[36]

While Bradford's work deals with global production patterns, business practices, and compliance with EU standards, the discussion becomes immediately political in the field of data privacy, where both the *de facto* and the *de jure* "Brussels Effect" can be observed. According to a study by Graham Greenleaf, European influence and standards by far have had the biggest impact on privacy laws outside Europe.[37] Over thirty non-European countries so far have adopted EU-style privacy laws.[38] The *Wall Street Journal* stated as early as 2003, "Privacy protection is another sign of the EU's growing influence as a trading bloc and its emergence as a regulatory superpower."[39] Greenleaf observed in 2012, "There is nothing occurring in the rest of the world which represents a coherent alternative to the spread of European-influenced data privacy standards, or even coherent resistance (except in the USA) to the adoption of such standards."[40] Steven C. Benett added, "Indeed, EU data policy developments have, to some degree, pushed the world toward uniform standards of data protection and have spurred U.S. regulators to action."[41] In the United States, the White House announced a plan for the Consumer Privacy Bill of Rights in February 2012, which, according to Anu Bradford, may suggest that the U.S. is coming around finally to embrace EU privacy standards.[42] Regardless of government actions, many private U.S. companies like Microsoft have already adopted de-facto the standards of EU privacy law for their global business operations.[43]

Paul M. Schwartz, however, disagrees that this is a result of the "Brussels Effect." He cites two reasons: the existence of certain EU policies that conflict with information privacy (notably contradictory member state policies) and limits on the EU's power in the global information economy.[44] He spe-

tory standards…with the overt aim of achieving efficiency."[46]

It is also worth noting that the United States has been very successful in expanding U.S. Extraterritoriality – the extension of U.S. federal law to activities outside the borders of the United States – with, for example, the Foreign Corrupt Practices Act of 1977 (FCPA) and its electronic discovery stipulations. The FCPA obliges U.S. foreign affiliates and selected non-US companies to provide electronic data even if the data resides outside the United States.[47] Yet as Professor Anthony J. Colangelo states:

> The law is complex without subtlety, knotted without development, and often blunt without judgment. (…) The law offers disturbingly little predictive assurance on how any given statute will be construed on any given set of facts not already squarely addressed by precedent.[48]

Thus, the FCPA can by no means be seen as a legal blueprint for other

The Snowden revelations puts substantial pressure on U.S. companies to convince European officials that they are complying with strict European standards, or they risk being shut out of the EU's common market.

cifically cites the case of the EU-U.S. negotiations over the EU's Data Protection Directive in 1994, which included bargaining rather than the EU unilaterally imposing its standards.[45] In his work, Schwartz prefers Anne-Marie Slaughter's "harmonization networks," where regulators "harmonize regula-

countries to adopt and it appears that the EU will by default be able to more efficiently push its legal agenda unilaterally rather than through Slaughter's "harmonization networks."

In the intermediate future, two factors are making the European Union a stronger unilateral player in the privacy field. First, the Edward Snowden's revelations of a U.S.-led global surveillance program created new political impetus for stronger data privacy laws in the EU and in the world while diminishing "U.S. soft power."[49] Second, the isolation of the United Kingdom—which

and Investment Partnership (TTIP): there is neither need nor justification to give way to any demands from the U.S. side to decrease the level of data protection in Europe. On the contrary, as the data protection commissioners in Germany and in

The sudden announcement by U.S. Attorney General Eric Holder that Europeans can sue over U.S. privacy rights violations is a strong indicator of the increasing strength of the "Brussels Effect" in setting data privacy standards.

has different data protection legislation from the continental member states of the EU based on common law—and its government under David Cameron, who unsuccessfully opposed the election of Jean-Claude Juncker as the new president of the European Commission, diminishes the UK's political influence in Brussels.

It is clear that the Snowden revelations vicariously have increased Brussels' political strengths in the data privacy debate within Europe and with the United States by putting the latter on the diplomatic defense. This could lead the EU to become more assertive during the negotiations of the new Transatlantic Trade and Investment Partnership agreement, which also deals with transatlantic data flows.[50] Alexander Dix, Commissioner for Data Protection and Freedom of Information of Berlin states:

> The European Union is in a rather comfortable position in the current negotiations with the U.S. government on a Transatlantic Trade

Europe have rightly suggested, the TTIP negotiations should be used by the EU Commission to convince the U.S. government of the need to introduce federal legislation for the better protection of personal data in the private sector. This could lead to a harmonised and level playing field in a future transatlantic free trade area.[51]

The European Parliament has already called on the European Commission to ensure that the TTIP does not weaken European data privacy standards. In addition, the EU Parliament called for a review of the Safe Harbor agreement, arguing that the agreement should be suspended because it cannot provide "adequate" protection based on the Data Protection Directive.[52] Both steps might be interpreted as symbolic gestures, but concrete evidence has emerged recently that the U.S. position is shifting.

In the past, the biggest stumbling blocks between Washington and Brussels have been that EU citizens do not enjoy privacy rights parity in the U.S. Privacy Act of 1974.[53] However, the sudden announcement by U.S. Attorney General Eric Holder in June 2014 that Europeans—subject to congressional approval—can sue over U.S. privacy rights violations is a strong indicator of the increasing strength of the "Brussels Effect" in setting data privacy standards since Washington has stalled negotiations on the subject for many years prior to the breaking of the NSA scandal.[54] Slaughter's "harmonization networks" fail to entirely explain the sudden turnaround of American negotiators.

In addition, internal developments within the EU may lead to more streamlined data privacy policies in EU member states. In the United Kingdom the interpretation and enforcement of the Data Protection Act of 1998 has lead to some of the weakest data privacy protection in the European Union; in fact some privacy rights groups have indicated that the Data Protection Directive has never been implemented properly in the country.[55] Moreover, there has been little political will to revise the law substantially in the UK as a report on the subject states, "There appears to be a continuing reluctance on the part of government to consider the possibility of widespread reform of the existing law so as to rationalize the existing piecemeal structure and create a single, comprehensive regulatory framework for surveillance and data collection."[56] Additionally, the UK government has repeatedly opposed reform of the EU Data Protection Directive.[57]

With the recent political defeat of David Cameron, who opposed the election of Jean-Claude Juncker as the president of the powerful European Commission, along with talk about a potential UK exit from the European Union as well as the introduction of a new system of qualified majority voting in the Council of the European Union, British ability to influence data protection reform is set to diminish in the intermediate future.[58] Juncker, a candidate from the European People's Party— the party that drove the reform of data protection rules—is committed to pushing for the new EU data privacy regulation.[59] As such, the diminishing influence of one of the principal opponents to the reform will alleviate some of the internal contradictory EU policies in data protection policies, which were cited by Schwartz as evidence of the weakness of the "Brussels's effect," and conversely strengthen it.

Conclusion. The European Union uses a strict regulation system that broadly affects EU member states' approaches to privacy, whereas the United States relies on a "patchwork" approach—sectoral laws combined with industry self-regulation. As outlined above, the Snowden revelations have made unilateral regulatory globalization— "The Brussels Effect"—more likely. The NSA scandal has put the U.S. government and U.S. companies at a diplomatic disadvantage during the EU-U.S. bilateral negotiations, which is being exploited by European companies and governments to further their own agendas. For example, the German government recently cancelled a deal with Verizon communications.[60] The U.S. cloud computing industry alone could lose between $21.5 billion and $35 billion over the next three years.[61] In addition, internal political dynamics within the EU—notably the diminishing influence of the United Kingdom—will result in more coherent EU data privacy rules. Fear of being shut out completely from European markets in the near term will pressure U.S. companies to comply more closely with EU standards, which will amplify the "Brussels Effect" globally.

Disclaimer: This article represents the views of the author and not necessarily those of the EastWest Institute.

NOTES

1 Steven C. Bennett, "The 'Right to Be Forgotten': Reconciling EU and US Perspectives," *Berkeley Journal of International Law* 30, no. 1 (2012): 169, Internet, http://scholarship.law.berkeley.edu/cgi/viewcontent.cgi?article=1429&context=bjil&sei-redir=1&referer=http%3A%2F%2Fscholar.google.com%2Fscholar_url%3Fhl%3Den%26q%3Dhttp%3A%2F%2Fscholarship.law.berkeley.edu%2Fcgi%2Fviewcontent.cgi%253Farticle%253D1429%2526context%253Dbjil%26sa%3DX%26scisig%3DAAGBfm0GvCQJZVB8GqjIx-vUkATNMCs75Q%26oi%3Dscholarr#search=%22http%3A%2F%2Fscholarship.law.berkeley.edu%2Fcgi%2Fviewcontent.cgi%3Farticle%3D1429%26context%3Dbjil%22 (date accessed: 29 June 2014).

2 Executive Office of the President, "Big Data: Seizing Opportunities, Preserving Data," Internet, http://www.whitehouse.gov/sites/default/files/docs/big_data_privacy_report_may_1_2014.pdf (date accessed: 30 June 2014): 16.

3 John Cassidy, "The Supreme Court Gets It Right on Cell-Phone Privacy," Internet, http://www.newyorker.com/online/blogs/johncassidy/2014/06/scotus-on-right-side-of-privacy-debate.html (date accessed: 29 June 2014).

4 The United States Department of Justice, "Privacy Act of 1974," Internet, http://www.justice.gov/opcl/privacy-act-1974 (date accessed: 28 June 2014). The eight pillars of the framework are outlined here: Appendix A – Fair Information Practice Principles (FIPPS) in "National Strategy for Trusted Entities in Cyberspace", Internet http://www.nist.gov/nstic/NSTIC-FIPPs.pdf (date accessed: 17 July 2014).

5 Paul M. Schwartz, "The EU-U.S. Privacy Collision: A Turn to Institutions and Procedures," Internet, http://scholarship.law.berkeley.edu/cgi/viewcontent.cgi?article=2906&context=facpubs (date accessed: 30 June 2014): 1970.

6 Neil M. Richards, "The Limits of Tort Privacy," Internet, http://jthtl.org/content/articles/V9I2/JTHTLv9i2_Richards.PDF (date accessed: 27 June 2014).

7 Tort Law: An Overview, "Legal Dictionary", Internet, http://www.law.cornell.edu/wex/tort (date accessed: 18 July 2014).

8 For a full list see: William Prosser, "Privacy", *California Law Review* 48, no. 3 (1960): pp.383-423, Internet, http://www.californialawreview.org/assets/pdfs/misc/prosser_privacy.pdf (date accessed: 17 July 2014).

9 Anu Bradford, "The Brussels Effect," *Northwestern University Law Review* 107, no. 1 (2012):23, Internet, https://www.law.northwestern.edu/lawreview/v107/n1/1/LR107n1Bradford.pdf (date accessed: 26 June 2014).

10 Schwartz, "The EU-U.S. Privacy Collision," 2013.

11 The United States Department of Justice, "Electronic Communications Privacy Act of 1986," Internet, http://www.justice.gov/jmd/ls/legislative_histories/pl99-508/pl99-508.html (date accessed: 27 June 2014).

12 The United States Department of Justice, "The Foreign Intelligence Surveillance Act of 1978," Internet, https://it.ojp.gov/default.aspx?area=privacy&page=1286 (date accessed: 28 June 2014).

13 Donald C. Dowling, "International Data Protection and Privacy Law," Internet, http://www.whitecase.com/files/publication/367982f8-6dc9-478e-ab2f-5fdf2d96f84a/presentation/publicationattachment/30c48c85-a6c4-4c37-84bd-6a4851f87a77/article_intldataprotectionandprivacylaw_v5.pdf (date accessed: 27 June 2014), 18-24.

14 Schwartz, "The EU-U.S. Privacy Collision," 1970.

15 Francesca Bignami, "European Versus American Liberty: A Comparative Privacy Analysis of Antiterrorism Data Mining," Internet, http://scholarship.law.duke.edu/cgi/viewcontent.cgi?article=2305&context=faculty_scholarship (date accessed: 30 June 2014), 634.

16 European Court of Human Rights, "European Convention on Human Rights," Internet, http://www.echr.coe.int/Documents/Convention_ENG.pdf (date accessed: 27 June 2014).

17 "Charter of Fundamental Rights of the European Union," Internet, http://www.europarl.europa.eu/charter/pdf/text_en.pdf (date accessed: 28 June 2014).

18 Human and Constitutional Rights Resources, "European Convention on Human Rights," Internet, http://www.hrcr.org/docs/Eur_Convention/euroconv3.html (date accessed: 29 June 2014), Article 8.

19 Didier Bigo, Sergio Carrera, Nicholas Hernanz, Julien Jeandesboz, Joanna Parkin, Francesco Ragazzi, Amandine Scherrer, "Mass Surveillance of Personal Data by EU Member States and Its Compatibility with EU Law," Internet, http://www.ceps.eu/book/mass-surveillance-personal-data-eu-member-states-and-its-compatibility-eu-law (date accessed: 28 June 2014), 19.

20 "Directive 95/46/EC of the European Parliament and of the Council of 24 October 1995 on the Protection of Individuals with Regard to the Processing of Personal Data and on the Free Movement of Such Data," Internet, http://eur-lex.europa.eu/LexUriServ/LexUriServ.do?uri=CELEX:31995L0046:en:HTML (date accessed: 30 June 2014).

21 Ibid, Article 8.

22 Schwartz, "The EU-U.S. Privacy Collision," 174.

23 European Commission, "Commission Proposes a Comprehensive Reform of the Data Protection Rules," Internet, http://ec.europa.eu/justice/newsroom/data-protection/news/120125_en.htm

NOTES

(date accessed: 29 June 2014).

24 European Parliament, "Q&A on EU data protection reform", Internet, http://www.europarl.europa.eu/news/en/news-room/content/20130502BKG07917/html/QA-on-EU-data-protection-reform (date accessed: 18 July 2014).

25 European Commission, "Fact Sheet on the 'Right to be Forgotten' Ruling, Internet, http://ec.europa.eu/justice/data-protection/files/factsheets/factsheet_data_protection_en.pdf (date accessed: 29 June 2014).

26 Laurent De Muyter, Jonathon Little, Mauricio F. Paez, Katherine S. Ritchey, Undine von Diemar, "European Parliament Votes in Favor of General Data Protection Regulation and Threatens Suspension of Data Transfers to U.S.," Internet, http://www.mondaq.com/unitedstates/x/302224/Data+Protection+Privacy/European+Parliament+Votes+In+Favor+Of+General+Data+Protection+Regulation+And+Threatens+Suspension+Of+Data+Transfers+To+US (date accessed: 27 June 2014).

27 Ralf Bosen, "Power Struggles Delay EU Data Protection Reform," Internet, http://www.dw.de/power-struggles-delay-eu-data-protection-reform/a-17631222 (date accessed: 30 June 2014).

28 Federal Trade Commission, "Remarks to the Mentor Group Forum for EU-US Legal-Economic Affairs, Internet, http://www.ftc.gov/sites/default/files/documents/public_statements/remarks-mentor-group-forum-eu-us-legal-economic-affairs-brussels-belgium/130416mentorgroup.pdf (date accessed: 30 June 2014).

29 European Commission, "Communication from the Commission to the European Parliament and the Council on the Functioning of the Safe Harbour from the Perspective of EU Citizens and Companies Established in the EU," Internet, http://ec.europa.eu/justice/data-protection/files/com_2013_847_en.pdf (date accessed: 29 June 2014).

30 Working Party, "Working Party on the Protection of Individuals with Regard to the Processing of Personal Data," Internet, http://ec.europa.eu/justice/data-protection/article-29/documentation/opinion-recommendation/files/1999/wp23_en.pdf (date accessed: 26 June 2014).

31 The author would like to thank the anonymous peer reviewer for this insightful comment.

32 Schwartz, "The EU-U.S. Privacy Collision," 1980.

33 Tom Jowitt, "Irish Court Asks EU to Review Facebook NSA Data Sharing," Internet, http://www.techweekeurope.co.uk/news/irish-court-data-sharing-nsa-review-147662 (date accessed: 29 June 2014).

34 Bradford, "The Brussels Effect," 3.

35 Ibid, 5.

36 Ibid, 6.

37 Ibid

38 Graham Greenleaf, "The Influence of European Data Privacy Standards Outside Europe: Implications for Globalisation of Convention 108," Internet, http://www.coe.int/t/dghl/standardsetting/dataprotection/Global_standard/GG_European_standards2010.pdf (date accessed: 27 June 2014), 23.

39 David Scheer, "Europe's New High-Tech Role: Playing Privacy Cop to World," Internet, http://online.wsj.com/news/articles/SB106574949477122300 (date accessed: 28 June 2014).

40 Greenleaf, "The Influence of European," 4.

41 Bennett, "The 'Right to Be Forgotten'," 177.

42 Bradford, "The Brussels Effect," 23.

43 Brad Smith, "Privacy Authorities Across Europe Approve Microsoft's Cloud Commitments," Internet, http://blogs.technet.com/b/microsoft_blog/archive/2014/04/10/privacy-authorities-across-europe-approve-microsoft-s-cloud-commitments.aspx (date accessed: 28 June 2014).

44 Schwartz, "The EU-U.S. Privacy Collision," 1990.

45 Ibid, 1985.

46 Ibid, 2013.

47 "Since 1977, the anti-bribery provisions of the FCPA have applied to all U.S. persons and certain foreign issuers of securities. With the enactment of certain amendments in 1998, the anti-bribery provisions of the FCPA now also apply to foreign firms and persons who cause, directly or through agents, an act in furtherance of such a corrupt payment to take place within the territory of the United States. The FCPA also requires companies whose securities are listed in the United States to meet its accounting provisions." The United States Department of Justice, "Foreign Corrupt Practices Act", Internet, http://www.justice.gov/criminal/fraud/fcpa/ (date accessed: Friday July 18, 2014).

48 Anthony J. Colangelo, "A Unified Approach to Extraterritoriality", *Virginia Law Review* 97, (2011), Internet, https://www.law.stanford.edu/sites/default/files/event/265497/media/slspublic/A_Unified_Approach_to-Extraterritoriality_1.pdf (date accessed: July 18 2014).

49 Andranik Migranyan, "Scandals Harm U.S. Soft Power," Internet, http://nationalinterest.org/commentary/scandals-harm-us-soft-power-8695 (date accessed: 27 June 2014).

50 Shayerah Ilias Akhtar and Vivian C. Jones, "Proposed Transatlantic Trade and Investment Partnership (T-TIP): In Brief," Internet, http://fas.org/sgp/crs/row/R43158.pdf (date accessed 29 June 2014).

51 Alexander Dix, Gregor Thusing, Johannes Traut, Laurits Christensen, Federico Etro, Susan Ariel Aaronson, and Rob Maxim, "EU Data Protection Reform: Opportunities and Concerns," Internet, http://www.intereconomics.eu/archive/year/2013/5/871/ (date accessed: 29 June 2014).

NOTES

52 Ian Brown, "The Feasibility of Transatlantic Privacy-Protective Standards for Surveillance," Internet, http://papers.ssrn.com/sol3/papers.cfm?abstract_id=2433912 (date accessed: 28 June 2014), 13.

53 The United States Department of Justice, "Privacy Act of 1974."

54 Matthew J. Schwartz, "U.S. Plan Would Boost EU Privacy Rights," Internet, http://www.bankinfosecurity.com/us-plan-would-boost-eu-privacy-rights-a-6991 (date accessed: 27 June 2014).

55 Open Rights Group, "Call for Evidence: Data Protection Act," Internet, https://www.openrightsgroup.org/ourwork/reports/call-for-evidence-data-protection-act (date accessed: 30 June 2014).

56 Charles Raab and Benjamin Goold, "Protecting Information Privacy," Internet, http://www.equalityhumanrights.com/sites/default/files/documents/research/rr69.pdf (date accessed: 27 June 2014).

57 Monica Horton, "Germany v Britain Tussle Over New EU Data Privacy Rules," Internet, http://www.iptegrity.com/index.php/european-union/privacy/899-germany-v-britain-tussle-over-new-eu-data-privacy-rules (date accessed: 30 June 2014). However, in 2012, the UK has instituted criminal sanctions for those that are found to be in breach of data protection law: a measure which is not in other EU Member State legislation.

58 Toby Helm, "Humiliating Defeat for David Cameron Pushes Britain Toward EU Exit," Internet, http://www.theguardian.com/world/2014/jun/28/cameron-eu-juncker-defeat-britain-exit (date accessed: 28 June 2014).

59 Jean-Claude Juncker, "EPP Manifesto," Internet, http://juncker.epp.eu/epp-manifesto?lang=en (date accessed: 27 June 2014). However, this has to be caveated by the fact that Mr Juncker might wish to sacrifice data protection reform on the altar of appeasing the UK. In addition, the EPP as a political bloc composed of a number of national parties might well change its mind.

60 Mark Scott, "Irked by N.S.A., Germany Cancels Deal with Verizon," Internet, http://www.nytimes.com/2014/06/27/business/angered-by-nsa-activities-germany-cancels-verizon-contract.html?m abReward=RI%3A5&action=click&pgtype=Homepage &region=CColumn&module=Recommendation&src =rechp&WT.nav=RecEngine (date accessed: 27 June 2014).

61 Jonah Force Hill, "The Growth of Data Localization Post-Snowden: Analysis and Recommendations for U.S. Policymakers and Business Leaders," Internet, http://papers.ssrn.com/sol3/papers.cfm?abstract_id=2430275 (date accessed: 29 June 2014), 5.

Good Cyber Governance

The Human Rights and Multi-Stakeholder Approach

Anja Mihr

Good cyber governance must establish a human rights-based approach for (1) more accountability, (2) more transparency, and (3) more participation by stakeholders through the use of cyber tools, such as the Internet and mobile devices. Moreover, good cyber governance fosters human rights and protects them through technology. Cyberspace, however, is a borderless public space in which individuals, regardless of their citizenship, nationality, ethnicity, political orientation, or gender communicate and interact. Individuals use cyberspace and the Internet to conduct business, make policies, and organize their private lives. Yet this space does not have any common rules or standards, a governance apparatus, or enforcement or control mechanisms that would protect and foster people's activities. Universal human rights norms and standards can serve as guidance and benchmarks for setting up governance regimes in cyberspace.

Through new technologies, cyberspace offers an environment that consists of many participants who have the ability to affect and influence each other. This space is transparent and neutral in its nature, but often defined, broadened, limited, or censored by the people who use it. Internet communication is often anonymous and used and shared

Anja Mihr is the Head of the Rule of Law program at The Hague Institute for Global Justice, and an Associate Professor at the Netherlands Institute of Human Rights at the University of Utrecht. She has held prominent academic positions in Germany, the United States, Italy, China, and the Netherlands, focusing on issues of rule of law, governance, human rights, and democratization.

with the public worldwide, which usually remains unknown to the individual Internet user; namely, each of us. We nonetheless share our most private and personal data with this anonymous audience. Today, this global, public community numbers around 2.7 billion Internet users. If cyberspace were a country, it would be the largest and most populated in the world, albeit one without any constitutions or government. This "space" has no legislative or otherwise democratic decision-making bodies. It has no police or law enforcement mechanism, let alone protection mechanism to safeguard human rights for all Internet citizens.

For the purpose of this article, I will therefore argue that (1) cyber governance does not need new human rights norms or standards, but rather new governing and monitoring regimes and enforcement mechanisms that guarantee and safeguard the human rights of all people who use cyberspace; (2) we need to identify all private, public, governmental, and international actors

Cyber Governance and Human Rights.

On one hand, the Internet and cyberspace can foster and enhance individuals' inclusive participation and access to politics and business, which they otherwise would not have. On the other hand, it can also exclude those who are Internet-illiterate or have difficulty accessing the Internet (e.g., children, aging people, and people without Internet-access). By sharing private information in cyberspace, billions of Internet users have already created virtual twin-identities in this new space, without ever having a chance to delete that information. Personal relationships and friendships through social networks such as Renren and Facebook can be seemingly anonymous and yet provide a vast amount of personal data; thus, it is a space for public privacy.[1] Businesses and enterprises, education and training, finances and economics, private correspondence, and even health and personal issues are now dealt with by anyone who seeks access to it in this endless space.[2] Ultimately,

If cyberspace were a country, it would be the largest and most populated in the world, albeit one without any constitutions or government.

who carry responsibilities in either violating or fostering human rights in the Internet; and (3) all users need to establish mechanisms that enhance trust in institutions (e.g., governments), companies (e.g., Internet providers, servers), and organizations (e.g., Facebook, YouTube).

what is missing in cyberspace is a quasi-government or governance regime that governs the needs and claims of its citizens through monitoring and enforcement bodies: a good cyber governance regime.

Although international governmental organizations (IGOs), such as the United Nations (UN), the Organization for American States (OAS), the

African Union (AU), and the European Union (EU) aim to set international standards and legally-binding treaties for the use of cyberspace and Internet to be respected and enforced by national governments, they generally fail to do so. The reason is that each state's powers and enforcement power often end at state borders because their mandate to protect human rights is entirely based on state sovereignty and governments. Also, IGOs and international courts often have limited measures and means to protect human rights, let alone enforce them.

Because cyberspace has no physical or national borders, the ways and means to govern this new borderless regime are not yet defined. Nevertheless, in the debate and effort to set up a cyberspace governance regime, human rights norms and standards -- such as the right to privacy, security, health, free expression, movement, and enterprise -- provide guidance to the various different actors that are involved in the regulatory design of the cyberspace regime. If established, the cyberspace governing body will consist of multiple stakeholders and actors. This includes national, international, as well as private actors such as representatives of companies, social networks, NGOs, and individuals. The World Internet Governance Forum under the UN has initiated such a concept.[3] Other fundamental freedoms and privacy human rights that are dealt with in this context are: freedom of expression, religion, political opinion, art, and written texts; free and equal access to information; and the protection of privacy issues such as family relations, friendships, and health issues. Furthermore, human rights in cyberspace is based upon secure protection from harassment and persecution on the Internet based on one's own political, ethical, or gender identity along with undisclosed professional, educational or health data. Cyber human rights should protect an individual's intellectual property and creativity in areas such as art, movies, pictures, literature, scientific results, etc. with access at any time to fair and open trials.

Good cyber governance has to be conducted over a domain of an individual's public privacy, which includes public and private data. It must reconcile the freedom of information and expression on the Internet with the security and privacy of individuals in cyberspace. According to international standards and definitions, privacy is a personal space in which we develop our personality in a confident and free way, exercise our skills and capacities, maintain our health, and enjoy social relationships with family and friends.[4] Hence, privacy in cyberspace means using the Internet as a service tool for private purposes without fearing that third parties, such as governments or companies (e.g., national security agencies, Google+, Microsoft) are accessing, selling, or publicly posting our data for national security or business purposes without our consent. Eventually, maintaining public privacy faces the challenge of how to balance our personal, professional, and private interests using the Internet as a free and open access communication tool, while creating standards and rules that may inhibit some level of privacy.

The debates and discussions around Internet freedom and privacy rights are fundamentally important in the areas of data protection, cybersecurity, cyber surveillance, and cyberwar through computer viruses. Some call it the "World Wide War" in which various state and non-state actors such as individual hackers are equally involved. Commercial-state or inter-governmental agreements, such as the Stop Online Piracy Act (SOPA), the NSA's surveillance program, PRISM, or the Anti-Counterfeiting Trade Agreement (ACTA), are just a few governmental initiatives to regain the control over the borderless dataflow. The challenge will be to assess how human rights can be fully guaranteed under these arrangements and agreements.

The often proclaimed 'right to Internet', which aims to allow individual access to the Internet at any time, and the right to be forgotten to ensure that one's own personal data remains private and can be deleted at any time, are already part of overall human rights standards concerning access to information, the right to privacy, and data protection (as in the EU Fundamental Rights Charter) and participation. The EU Court of Justice passed a landmark decision in May 2014 that buttresses privacy and the right of users to have their data removed or forgotten from the Internet. The ruling targets search engines and data providers such as Google, YouTube, and Facebook.[5] Unfortunately, it only applies to the EU territorial space.

A global solution has yet to come. The Research Division of the European Court of Human Rights has already made some headway in 2011 by publishing a groundbreaking document on potential case law concerning data protection and retention issues relevant for the Internet. However, other international or domestic courts might take some time in interpreting the legal rights laid down by the EU Court of Justice.[6]

Human rights are often inscribed and enforced by treaties, customary international law, general principles, and other sources of international law.[7] They include obligations and duties of governments, companies, individuals, or other legal entities (duty bearers) to act in certain ways or to refrain from certain acts. Human rights are often described as social, civil, economic, political, or cultural rights, and there is no hierarchy among them. These different categories of human rights cannot be exercised or enjoyed without one another. The human right to information, for example, applies to the extent that this information does not violate the dignity or privacy of others. This is the holistic approach to human rights under the principle of the Golden Rule: "Do no harm to others that which you would not want done to you."[8] Along these lines, a cyber human rights regime ought to be balanced and estimated insofar as they do not infringe on the rights of others.

That being said, protection of data should never justify censorship or random surveillance of individuals. Finding the balance depends very much on who decides the limits and borders of freedom of information. The more stakeholders involved, the more likely the resulting balance will be accepted. Ultimately, the UN Human Rights Council reminded us in 2012 that human rights are all valid both online and offline, and there is no difference whether they are violated in cyberspace or physical space within borders.[9] Yet the open question remains: who is the duty bearer? That is to say, who can protect, implement, and enforce human rights in cyberspace, if government authorities end at their state borders?

In 2013, the issues of cyber espionage and misuse of private data came about through the NSA affair between the United States, Germany, and Brazil. The former NSA contractor, Edward Snowden, revealed the U.S. government's warrantless and limitless surveillance of U.S. citizens and Internet users around the world.[10] The United States is now charging Snowden under the U.S. Espionage Act, but Snowden remains in exile in Russia while the

sensitive communications no longer take place online. Facebook users have become alarmed at posting private pictures online, and millions of users no longer send their e-mails unencrypted. The need for technical tools such as encryption and deciphering technology are highly demanded. In Europe alone, the number of encrypted data transferred rose in 2014 from 1.5% to 6.0%. Yet overall Snowden's revelations demonstrated that the problems of global surveillance — conducted by most NSAs in this world — need global answers, not just national or regional ones, let alone technical ones. The many national laws passed over the past year regarding data protection can only create more time, but not deliver the solution. Meanwhile, private, govern-

Snowden's revelations demonstrated that the problems of global surveillance — conducted by most NSAs in this world — need global answers, not just national or regional ones, let alone technical ones.

U.S. government works on extradition. Snowden's revelations continue to strongly impact the debate about privacy and its insufficient legal development and heavily violated laws. Even though the UN, the EU, and many nations extensively fine-tuned their laws and regulations on data protection in 2013, the main issue remains unresolved: how can privacy and freedom rights be safeguarded in cyberspace, if at all? Individually, many users started to adapt and become more cautious. Consequently, self-censorship by users could not be avoided and many

mental, and non-governmental actors have to discuss and decide which will be the common cyber-rules, standards and governance mechanisms that will end anarchy in cyberspace in the near future.

In response to these and other revelations, the UN Special Rapporteur on Freedom of Expression Frank de la Rue highlighted the fact that privacy and freedom of expression are interlinked and mutually dependent. Therefore, without adequate legislation and legal standards to ensure the privacy, security, and anonymity of communications, journalists, human rights defenders, and whistleblowers, it cannot be assured that their communications will not be subject to states' security uses.[11]

Efforts to tame cyberspace and establish overall rules and regulations to which we should all adhere to is as old as the cyberspace and Internet itself. In 1996, Jon Perry Barlow published the "Declaration of Independence of Cyberspace," indicating the situations and controversies that today's Internet users worldwide are worried about.[12] Barlow recognized twenty years ago that the Internet community, and thus the global user community, has to develop its own social contracts to determine how to handle its problems based on the Golden Rule, which is the foundation for realizing human rights. Whether or not such social contracts for cyberspace will ever be realized, the idea behind them is individual responsibility and adherence to human rights, which we, as members of the global community (whether private or public), have long agreed to. So-called 'digital rights' are already embedded in freedom rights, such as those stated in the Universal Declaration on Human Rights (UDHR) or the International Covenant on Civil and Political Rights (ICCPR). These rights allow the access and use of information and communications technology, like computers and digital media, to enhance any of the aforementioned human rights and the overall human right to information.[13] Consequently on December 10, 2013, the International Human Rights Day celebrated 65 years after the UDHR was proclaimed by the UN, over 500 writers and Noble Prize winners signed a petition urging the UN to draft an international bill on digital rights.[14] The massive support from the user community to develop such a concept is expected to impact the development of global Internet governance principles.

Internet Governance Principles and the Multi-stakeholder Approach.

In April 2014 in Sao Paulo, Brazil, various international organizations and stakeholders promoted the concept of Internet governance principles based on the multi-stakeholder approach. It promotes and protects the use of cyberspace and the Internet as a "platform for social, economic and human development and a catalyser to exercise human rights of all people of the world."[15] This approach requires the inclusive participation of all relevant actors, institutions, and organizations that deal with cyber governance. This can be a set of different private and public actors, such as Google, Yahoo, Facebook, the International Telecommunication Union (ITU), and governmental representatives and experts. This multi-stakeholder approach — if applied thoroughly — has the advantage that all relevant actors can participate and be heard on an equal basis. They not only vote or decide on subject matters together, but they also commit themselves to the successful implementation of the agreed subject matters. Ideally, they set their own standards and rules, defining possible repercussions or penalties for non-compliance by the involved stakeholders. Enforcement still relies heavily on cooperation with state actors, such as national security agencies, but can also be conducted by private actors through means of public 'cyber-pressure', utilizing naming and shaming tactics which may threaten the legitimacy of the respective company, state agency or otherwise. It will not fully replace state agencies -- and it never will -- but it leads more to individual and corporate responsibility. All actors involved jointly monitor, safeguard and enforce the jointly agreed rules and regulations. The 2005 World Summit on the Information Society's Tunis Agenda indicates some of the criteria for the multi-stakeholder approach. One example is whether member states and Cyber Security Organizations (CSOs) can call upon all stakeholders to ensure respect for privacy and the protection of personal information and data, through adoption of legislation, the implementation of collaborative frameworks, best practices, and self-regulatory and technological measures by business and users. They attach great importance to the multi-stakeholder implementation of decisions, which is explicitly mentioned in the Agenda.[16]

Regimes and organizations governed only by governmental stakeholders will lose legitimacy and thus effectiveness over the long run because they do not include citizens, companies, and organizations that struggle with applying human rights to cyberspace. During the 2012 UN governmental-run ITU world summit, authoritarian regimes often outnumbered democratic ones. As a result, they undercut the flexibility of the "multi-stakeholder" approach. Votes during these types of meetings disadvantage "democratic" governments, because democratic regimes are accountable to their electorate, whereas authoritarian ones often represent the interests of small group of elites only,

but not general citizens and Internet users in their country.[17]

Furthermore, good cyber governance requires free, open, and easy access for all citizens globally, although less than 30% of world population has regular access to the Internet. Recent statistics show that countries with high levels of social capital and technical infrastructures use E-Governance to run business or public affairs mainly through the Internet, unlike countries with fewer infrastructures.[18] In particular, E-Democracy that aims to have Internet-based general elections requires equal, safe and free access for all citizens under each respective political regime. The aim of inclusive participation via Internet can result in common agreements, norms, rules, and laws to govern communities. Countries that have high E-Democracy scores are also democratically mature in general.[19] Yet there is no evidence found that E-Democracy leverages democratic behavior in countries that generally score low in democracy or are governed in an autocratic manner. Because E-Democracy is just one way to build on already existing good governance principles such as accountability and responsiveness, transparency, and Internet citizen participation, there is no automatic causality between Internet access and democracy. But access to Internet, which enhances access to information and civic participation, can be a tool or catalyst to trigger cultural changes that eventually lead to more democratic ways to govern a society.

The core question remains, whether or not people can develop trust and confidence in these Internet tools that in return leverage the legitimacy of institutions or organizations that provide them — may they be public or private. In order to draw a correlation, we take a look at the general definition of democracy: the rule of the people for the people, which also describes the concept of rule of law as the basis for any democratic regime today. It becomes evident that cyber-technology, search engines, network providers, etc., can be used as tools or catalysts, but do not automatically lead to a democratic culture or country. Nonetheless, everyone who moves in cyberspace has the responsibility to protect and respect private data and freedom of information. We need common rules and standards, as well as strong decision-making, enforcement, and compliance mechanisms to realize good cyber governance. Internet users, providers, companies, and governments alike should be held responsible for both violating rights and protecting them.

Human Rights and Rule of Law.

Governmental authorities and democratic institutions are instrumental to safeguarding human rights in cyberspace. National and international courts also play a crucial role as part of this cyber regime to protect human rights. In a 2012 case concerning Turkey, the European Court of Human Rights (ECHR) reinforced the right of individuals to access the Internet by ruling against wholesale blocking of online content, asserting that the Internet has now become one of the principal means of exercising the right to freedom of expression and information.[20] In October 2013, the ECHR ruled that an Estonian news portal, Delfi, was responsible for offensive

anonymous posts against a ferry company. Previously, Estonia's Supreme Court ruled that the website owner was responsible for the comments, not the people who made them. The judges in Strasbourg backed that stance in 2013.[21] This means that service providers or website owners will be held accountable when their users or visitors post inappropriate language on their websites that violates the dignity and privacy of others. This has subsequently led to more surveillance and responsibility of owners on what is posted on their websites.

Legitimacy of any institution, company, or organization is achieved through the level of civic engagement or interaction in setting up, adhering to, or accepting common rules and standards. It increases or decreases by the level of Internet users' trust in or engagement with these entities. The more these entities comply with its commands and human rights, the higher their legitimacy will be. Therefore, these entities will enjoy a greater degree of legitimacy when applying good governance principles in businesses, governments, and CSOs, both online and offline.[22]

In the case of cyberspace, globalization and constructivist approaches help us understand why some argue that human rights norms diffusion impacts the way we think about national jurisdiction, state borders, and the nation-state. The global cyber governance regime is legitimate and sovereign if we interact on different levels.[23] The International Court of Justice (ICJ) has argued that territorial sovereignty also implies obligations to protect human rights in cyberspace. For example, if technical companies or servers violate human rights, they would be subject to national human rights laws, because even cyberspace requires the existence of some physical architecture.[24] In response to the debate on whether Internet can weaken or strengthen sovereignty and legitimacy of state institutions, UN Special Rapporteur de la Rule

users. Equal and universal legal standards are missing; thus, the claim for rule of law is one to be considered. International jurisdiction, customary and international human rights law, and the shifting role of duty bearer and rights holder towards more individual responsibility are all part of the recent

Legislation must stipulate that state surveillance of private communications must only occur under the most exceptional circumstances and exclusively under the supervision of an independent judicial authority.

recommended states review national laws regulating surveillance and update and strengthen laws and legal standards. Communications surveillance should be regarded as a highly intrusive act that potentially interferes with the rights to freedom of expression and privacy and threatens the foundation of a democratic society. Legislation must stipulate that state surveillance of private communications must only occur under the most exceptional circumstances and exclusively under the supervision of an independent judicial authority.[25]

Good Cyber Governance. Ultimately, human rights-oriented cyber governance is a new trend in which global Internet users aim to uphold their basic human rights through good cyber-governance principles. Yet there is no global rule of law culture in cyberspace as of yet, let alone any monitoring or enforcement mechanism based on the multi-stakeholder approach that would safeguard the rights of Internet

development towards an open and fair cyber governance regime.

While there is no lack of human rights standards or laws, the measures and mechanisms that allow us to comply and adhere to these standards are national, not global. This is where change has to take place. Therefore, the global cyber regime has to develop innovative ways and mechanisms to monitor and enforce global human rights standards that go beyond existing national measures. There might be different ways to do so without excluding existing legal or political mechanisms.

One suggestion that has been proposed in this article is the multi-stakeholder approach. The multi-stakeholder community of organizations, governments, and experts ought to frame existing common global guidelines and laws for the needs and purposes of Internet users. This might more likely guarantee the inclusion of the public Internet users and the protection of our privacy; namely, our civic and social human rights. A non-legally binding UN Resolution from December 2013 or the Internet governance principles promoted at NETMundial in Sao Paulo in 2014 indicate that governments emphasize preventing illegal surveillance and interception of private communications, and the illegal collection of personal data.[26] These highly intrusive acts violate the right to privacy and freedom of expression and may threaten the foundations of a democratic society. With UN resolution 192, member states recall their own obligations to ensure that measures taken to coun-

terterrorism or other security threats comply with international human rights law. Therefore, all governments of the world, in theory, aim to put an end to violations of these rights, and they are called to establish multi-stakeholder mechanisms with independent oversight, capable of ensuring transparency and accountability of state surveillance and interception of private communications and collection of personal data. It is vital to produce this new rule of law in cyberspace.

NOTES

1 A. Mihr (2013) Public Privacy-Human Rights in Cyberspace, Working Paper, Utrecht University, see: http://www.anjamihr.com/resources/Public+Privacy-WP-AnjaMihr$5B1$5D.pdf

2 Mindaugas Kiskis (2011) Entrepreneurship in Cyberspace: What do we know?, Social Technologies, Mykolas Romeris University, 1 (1), 37-48. http://www.doaj.org/doaj?func=fulltext&aId=1045782

3 Internet Governance Forum http://www.intgovforum.org/cms/

4 Helen Nissenbaum, "Toward an Approach to Privacy in Public: Challenges of Information Technology (1997) 7 (3), Ethics & Behavior, 207-219. http://www.nyu.edu/projects/nissenbaum/papers/toward_an_approach.pdf

5 Court of Justice of the European Union (May 2014), Factsheet about Right to be Forgotten ruling C 131/12 http://ec.europa.eu/justice/data-protection/files/factsheets/factsheet_data_protection_en.pdf ; and Press Release http://curia.europa.eu/jcms/upload/docs/application/pdf/2014-05/cp140070en.pdf

6 Council of Europe, ECHR, Research Division (2011) "Internet: Case-law of the European Court of Human Rights, Strasbourg, June 2011 www.echr.coe.int. (Access December 2013).

7 UN Doc. General Assembly Resolution 217 A (III). Preamble of the Universal Declaration of Human Rights. 18 December 1948.

8 Internet Encyclopedia of Philosophy, The Golden Rule, 2010 http://www.iep.utm.edu/goldrule/ (Access December 2013)

9 UN Doc. Doc. A/HRC/20/L.13. Human Rights Council, "The promotion, protection and enjoyment of human rights on the Internet," 29 June 2012, para.1.

10 Summary of Edward Snowden's NSA revelation in 2013: http://www.infoplease.com/news/2013/edward-snowden-leaks.html

11 UN Doc. A/HRC/23/40. Report of the Special Rapporteur on the promotion and protection of the right to freedom of opinion and expression, Frank La Rue, 17 April 2013, para.79.

12 John Perry Barlow, "A Declaration of the Independence of Cyberspace" 8 February 1996. https://projects.eff.org/~barlow/Declaration-Final.html (Access December 2013).

13 Office of the High Commissioner for Human Rights, Human Rights Indicators: A Guide to Measurement and Implementation (Geneva: 2013) https://unp.un.org/Details.aspx?pid=23745 (Access December 2013); For the definition of digital rights see: Business and Human Rights Resource Center, "Ranking Digital Rights project:" http://www.business-humanrights.org/Documents/Ranking_Digital_Rights (Access December 2013).

14 The Guardian, International bill of digital rights: call from 500 writers around the world (10 December 2013) http://www.theguardian.com/world/2013/dec/10/international-bill-digital-rights-petition-text (Access December 2013).

15 European Commission (2014), Input on "Internet Governance Principles," NETMundial, Sao Paulo 23-24 April 2014, http://content.netmundial.br/files/176.pdf

16 World Summit Information Society Tunis Agenda (2005) http://www.itu.int/wsis/docs2/tunis/off/6rev1.html

17 Multi-stakeholder approach for cyber-security, read more at http://www.project-syndicate.org/commentary/joseph-s--nye-contrasts-multilateral-

NOTES

and--multi-stakeholder--approaches-to-governing-cyberspace#3tHlru7sIjTo2Qsf.99

18 United Nations, E-Government Survey 2012. E-Government for the people (New York: 2012), 9ff. http://unpan1.un.org/intradoc/groups/public/documents/un/unpan048065.pdf (Access December 2013).

19 Irina Netchaeva "E-Government and E-Democracy. A Comparison of Opportunities in the North and South"(2002) 64 The International Journal for Communications Studies 467-477.

20 ECHR, Case Yildirim v.Turkey, 18 December 2012, para.54.

21 ECHR, Case Delfi As v. Estonia,10 October 2013.

22 Jonathan Weinberg, "Non-State Actors and Global Informal Governance — The Case of ICANN," in Thomas Christiansen and Christine Neuhold (eds.) International Handbook on Informal Governance (Massachusetts: Edward Elgar Publishing, 2012) http://jotwell.com/exploring-legitimacy-in-Internet-institutions/ (Access December 2013).

23 Wolff Heintschel von Heinegg, "Legal Implications of Territorial Sovereignty in Cyberspace" (2012) 4 International Conference on Cyber Conflict, 7-19 http://www.ccdcoe.org/publications/2012proceedings/1_1_von_Heinegg_LegalImplicationsOfTerritorialSovereigntyInCyberspace.pdf (Access December 2013).

24 Wolff Heintschel von Heinegg, "Territorial Sovereignty and Neutrality in Cyberspace" (2013) 89 International Law Studies, 123-156 http://www.usnwc.edu/getattachment/ff9537ce-94d6-49a8-a9ef-51e335126c1e/von-Heinegg.aspx (Access December 2013); Wolff Heintschel von Heinegg, "Legal Implications of Territorial Sovereignty in Cyberspace" p.15-17. http://www.ccdcoe.org/publications/2012proceedings/1_1_von_Heinegg_LegalImplicationsOfTerritorialSovereigntyInCyberspace.pdf (Access December 2013).

25 UN Doc. A/HRC/23/40. Report of the Special Rapporteur on the promotion and protection of the right to freedom of opinion and expression, Frank La Rue, 17 April 2013, para.81 http://www.ohchr.org/Documents/HRBodies/HRCouncil/RegularSession/Session23/A.HRC.23.40_EN.pdf (Access December 2013).

26 UN Doc. A/C.3/68/L.45. General Assembly, "The right to privacy in the digital age," 1 November 2013.

Detaching Internet Governance from the State

Globalizing the IANA

Milton Mueller

Milton Mueller is a professor at the Syracuse University School of Information Studies. For the past 15 years, his research, teaching, and public service have focused on the political economy of communication and global Internet governance.

Sixteen years after it was created, the Internet Corporation for Assigned Names and Numbers (ICANN) is once again at the center of a global controversy. The U.S. Commerce Department holds a special form of leverage over ICANN known as the IANA Functions Contract.[1] The contract gives the U.S. government control over who is the central authority for coordinating Internet identifiers such as domain names. In March of 2014, the Commerce Department announced that it would eliminate its contractual oversight of ICANN and put it completely in the hands of the "global multistakeholder community."

The IANA transition raises fascinating questions about the Internet and global governance. To what extent can we detach Internet governance from the state and situate governance authority in truly autonomous, Internet-centric institutions? Without the tether to the U.S. government, to whom will ICANN be accountable? Could ICANN's central role in Internet coordination be taken over or abused without the U.S. backstop? This is yet another instance of how Internet governance challenges traditional state-based institutions.

This paper analyzes the IANA transition from a global

governance perspective. It first provides an explanation of what the IANA functions really are and what the U.S. role in them has been. The paper explores the international relations dimension of the transition, showing how it fits into the ongoing contest between the 'multistakeholder' model of Internet governance and state-centric Internet governance. In the course of this exposition, the paper critically assesses the claim that the IANA transition threatens Internet freedom or risks 'losing' the Internet to authoritarian states. Finally, the paper proposes a model for the transition that minimizes key risks and keeps ICANN accountable.

U.S. Policy: Globalization through Privatization. The Internet protocols were developed primarily by researchers in the United States, supported first by the Department of Defense and then by the National Science Foundation and other education and research networks in the U.S., Europe, and Asia. After about 10 years, the Internet protocols became

tional forms of governance were perceived as undesirable — not only by the U.S. government, but also by the techies who developed the net and the mostly U.S.-based businesses who gravitated to it. Congressional legislation was perceived as narrowly partisan and special interest-driven — inappropriate for a global medium. For much the same reasons, letting scores of parliaments in other countries legislate would erect jurisdictional barriers to the naturally global scope of data communication. An international treaty would take years to negotiate and would risk subjecting the Internet to economic regulations designed to protect vested interests, leading to weaker free expression guarantees.

The Clinton Administration responded to these challenges with decisive and innovative measures. It established a framework for non-governmental administration of the domain name system (DNS).[3] A nonprofit corporation would govern the DNS by means of private contracts and bottom-up policy development. The funda-

ICANN's legitimacy suffered. It was widely perceived as accountable not to the global Internet community but primarily to the U.S. government.

the globally dominant data communication standard, providing a platform for billions of dollars in e-commerce, media and services. It was clear that the legacy governance arrangements had to change.

But how does one govern the global Internet? This was a topic of much debate in the mid-1990s.[2] Most tradi-

mental logic underlying their approach was what I call globalization through privatization. The 1998 Department of Commerce National Telecommunications and Information Administration (NTIA) white paper setting the policy framework for ICANN declared that:

In withdrawing the U.S. Government from DNS management and promoting the establishment of a new, non-governmental entity to manage Internet names and addresses, a key U.S. Government objective has been to ensure that the increasingly global Internet user community has a voice in decisions affecting the Internet's technical management.[4]

In other words, the U.S. 'internationalized' the governance of Internet identifiers by delegating authority to a private sector non-profit. Global governance would occur by means of private contracts that reflected policies made by a new, sui generis multi-stakeholder process open to anyone in the world. The strategy of globalization-through-privatization resonated with the cosmopolitan Internet technical community, which had self-governed the Internet for the previous 20 years. But it also had substantial support from business interests and rights-oriented civil society groups, who favored direct participation in an open regime over indirect, state-led representation in intergovernmental institutions.

The white paper promised that the U.S. supervisory role would disappear within two years (i.e., by 2000). But for a number of reasons, the U.S. failed to complete the transition. For 16 years, ICANN remained a U.S. government contractor rather than an independent, multi-stakeholder governance institution. Because of that, ICANN's legitimacy suffered. It was widely perceived as accountable not to the global Internet community but primarily to the U.S. government.

The Structure of the Present System.
It is important to understand the actual mechanisms by which the U.S.

exercises its unilateral control. The IANA functions are diagrammed in Figure 1 and described below.

The first role is global policy maker for the DNS. This role is occupied by ICANN and its policy development process. Formally recognized by the U.S. in 1999 as the "NewCo" called for in the 1998 White Paper, ICANN makes policies that regulate domain name registries and registrars in the generic top-level domains, and determines what new top-level domains go into the root zone file.

The second role is that of the IANA Functions Operator. The IANA functions, as noted before, are defined by a U.S. Commerce Department contract that has been awarded to ICANN. Thus, the IANA is a department within ICANN. But the contract bars IANA staff from influencing the policy making process; IANA is only supposed to implement policies adopted by ICANN.

The third role is the political oversight function, referred to as the "Administrator" in the IANA functions contract. The Administrator role is currently held by the NTIA. When ICANN requests changes, additions or deletions to the root zone file, the IANA first transmits them to the NTIA for approval. Of course, NTIA also has the power to define the terms of the IANA contract and the power to award it.

The fourth role is the Root Zone Maintainer. This is performed by Verisign, Inc. under a Cooperative Agreement with NTIA. Changes approved by the NTIA are sent to VeriSign (or any successor entity designated by the Commerce Department), which actually edits the root zone data, cryptographi-

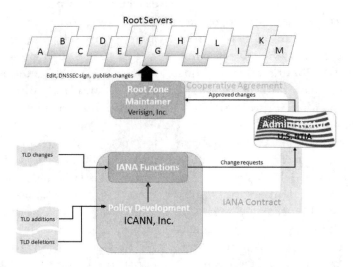

Figure 1 Internet Root Zone Gvernance Structure

cally signs it, and distributes the resulting content to the root server operators.[5] Once the data is published via the root server operators, the information maps specific domain names to specific internet protocol addresses, allowing anyone in the world to communicate with anyone else on the Internet using a globally unique domain name.

Significance of U.S. control. It is common to assert that the special U.S. role doesn't matter because it has always taken the role of a neutral steward. But this is not quite true. The IANA contract does far more than empower the NTIA to passively bless whatever changes ICANN makes to the root zone. It also regulates ICANN's behavior in some detail. For example, it requires ICANN to be incorporated in, maintain a physical address in, and perform the IANA functions in the U.S., making IANA and ICANN subject to U.S.

law. It also provides America with greater political influence over ICANN. The need to regularly renew the contract and the fact that NTIA is funded by the U.S. Congress, which can threaten to cut its budget or pass legislation affecting it, all provide the U.S. with outsized influence over ICANN. Not only can the U.S. threaten to award the contract to someone else, it has carte blanche to modify the contract to shape ICANN's behavior in unforeseen ways.

The extent of U.S. control was demonstrated during the controversy over a proposed .xxx domain for adult content in 2005. The Bush administration NTIA caved in to domestic political pressure and threatened to block entry of the domain into the root after ICANN had approved it.[6] Even if this had never happened, the U.S. role has a major, ongoing impact on the autonomy and integrity of the ICANN policy development process.[7] ICANN's dependence on one government clearly contradicts the norm of a globalized, open, multi-stakeholder Internet governance in which all stakeholders participate on equal footing in a fair process.

The IANA Transition and International Relations. The initial creation of a new, globalized governance regime for the Internet relied heavily on the ability of the United States, with its decisive lead in early Internet development, to act both unilaterally and with global effect. But while that may have been necessary to put the regime into place, the retention of this special power for 16 years has undermined the legitimacy of the multistakeholder approach. Foreign Internet users see this — ostensibly nongovernmental but under the authority of one government — as a double standard. The IANA contract was always Exhibit A in complaints that multi-stakeholder governance was merely a fig leaf for U.S. dominance. A 2011 study of Domain Name System security initiated by the Department of Homeland Security identified a risk that "nation-states may want to capitalize on the perceived control of the United States over the Internet by offering a competing authoritative root (resulting in Internet fragmentation) to undermine the perceived hegemony of the United States."[8]

Predictably, unilateral U.S. oversight of ICANN was the subject of intense criticism during the World Summit on the Information Society (WSIS) from 2003 — 2005.[9] While American politicians and media dismissed much of this criticism as an attempt by authoritarian states to control the Internet, young democracies such as South Africa, India and Brazil, as well as member states of the European Commission, were all deeply uncomfortable with unilateral U.S. authority. Indeed, in this early period of Internet governance, nearly all states, including European democracies, were pushing for the pre-eminence of state actors in the formation of public policy for the Internet. Though Western states have generally aligned behind ICANN, the rivalry between multi-stakeholder and multilateral governance has continued, breaking out again during the December 2012 World Conference on International Telecommunications (WCIT) hosted by the ITU.[10]

As a result of this contest, the U.S. has allowed itself to be drawn into a game that gradually empowers governments at the expense of the multistakeholder model. In order to convince other governments of ICANN's legitimacy and desirability, the U.S. has strengthened the influence of ICANN's Governmental Advisory Committee (GAC). The GAC is a one country, one representative body — a kind of mini-United Nations — within ICANN. Although it is still nominally an advisory body whose advice can be rejected by the ICANN board, the U.S. government's quest to find acceptance for ICANN in the international community has made the GAC increasingly influential. Governments have been allowed, even encouraged, to use the GAC to completely rewrite or even veto policy decisions made by ICANN's bottom-up process.[11]

The Catalyst for Change. For many years, changing the IANA arrangement

was politically impossible. The Bush Administration reacted defensively to attacks on the U.S. role during WSIS, issuing a 2005 statement of "DNS Principles" that equated U.S. unilateral control with the "security and stability of the domain name system." The statement implied that it would "maintain its historic role in authorizing changes or modifications to the authoritative root zone file" forever.[12]

But Edward Snowden's exposure of globalized Internet surveillance by the U.S. National Security Agency (NSA) broke that logjam. It did so not because the U.S. lost its 'moral authority' and therefore chose to shamefacedly release its grip on IANA. No, the underlying calculus was far more practical. The Snowden revelations made it blindingly clear that the scale and scope of U.S. power over the digital environment vastly exceeded that of any other state. They also made it appear as if the global dominance of U.S. businesses in Internet services enhanced its military and intelligence superiority. Private sector services that were once perceived as relatively benign products of multinational corporations suddenly gained a national, quasi-militarized identity. The Snowden revelations thus could be used, and were used, to justify nationalistic regulation, data localization initiatives and boycotts of American companies. This backlash contained a serious threat to the global nature of the Internet itself. And though U.S. control of ICANN had nothing to do with the NSA's surveillance program, and NSA spying had nothing to do with ICANN, both were instances of an exceptional, wholly globalized form of power over the Internet held exclusively by the U.S.

government. It was therefore inevitable, and not at all unfair, for the two to be linked politically. In short, the surveillance scandal forced a choice: either be consistent about our commitment to the principle of globalization through privatization, or risk discrediting that governance model through its association with U.S. political and military hegemony.

It should not be surprising, therefore, that the most resounding linkage between the Snowden revelations and U.S. control of IANA came not from critics of multistakeholder governance - not from Russia or China - but from the leaders of the Internet's own governance institutions. In October 2013, the Directors of all the major Internet organizations — ICANN, the Internet Engineering Task Force, the Internet Architecture Board, the World Wide Web Consortium, the Internet Society, and all five of the regional Internet address registries — issued the Montevideo Statement.[13] The widely circulated statement warned against "Internet fragmentation at a national level" and expressed "strong concern over the undermining of the trust and confidence of Internet users globally due to recent revelations of pervasive monitoring and surveillance." As part of this statement, the leaders called for "the globalization of ICANN and IANA functions, towards an environment in which all stakeholders, including all governments, participate on an equal footing." This was a clear signal that it was time to end the special U.S. role. Five months later, after intensive but secret interagency consultations with ICANN and other Internet organizations, the Commerce Department announced its "intent to transition key Internet domain name functions" in order to "support and enhance the multistakeholder model of Internet policymaking and governance."[14]

The U.S. Congress Reacts. It was perhaps inevitable that the IANA transition, which should have happened a decade ago, would be interpreted in certain parts of Washington as "giving away the Internet." The nationalistic reaction is a classic example of why the state — any state — is inherently incapable of getting global Internet governance right. Key governance functions are perceived as instruments of national power or prestige; something that gives one government a strategic or com-

IANA transition provoked several legislative proposals in Congress to stop or delay it. The justifications for the legislation contained many bizarre claims. Republican advocates of 'limited government' were suddenly clamoring for continued government control over a critical aspect of Internet operations.[15] The NTIA's control of the IANA functions contract was lauded as a bulwark of Internet freedom. Its withdrawal from that role was said to risk putting the entire Internet into the hands of the Russians, the Chinese, or the ITU.

These arguments have no merit. To begin with, moving governance of the domain name system away from government and into the private sector is the linchpin of U.S. policy and the

The Snowden revelations made it blindingly clear that the scale and scope of U.S. power over the digital environment vastly exceeded that of any other state.

petitive advantage over others. National political pressures by their very nature reward politicians who seek special advantages and powers for domestic stakeholders and constituencies; they do not reward those who pursue a global public good. Yet what the Internet needs is a neutral and global public governance institution that receives input from all stakeholders and provides rules and decision making procedures that facilitate an orderly growth and evolution of data communications. To support the global Internet, governance needs to be denationalized.

The NTIA's announcement of the

entire rationale for creating ICANN in the first place. The IANA transition merely carries this longstanding policy to its logical conclusion. The idea that ending U.S. control opens the door to intergovernmental control is literally an inversion of the truth. The IANA transition removes DNS governance from governmental hands, and permanently lodges it in non-state actors in the Internet user and supplier community. The conditions NTIA set for the transition explicitly exclude turning it over to an intergovernmental institution or government-led system. If anything risks intergovernmental takeover efforts, it is the Congressional intervention itself. Nothing could do more to encourage renewed efforts at intergovernmental or national control of the DNS than the sight of the U.S. Congress asserting that 'the internet is ours.'

Those who voice fears of an "ITU takeover" or, even less plausibly, a "Putin takeover" or "Chinese takeover" of the root are unable to provide plausible scenarios by which this could happen. The absence of NTIA in the root zone modification loop doesn't make successful ratification of an intergovernmental treaty regulating ICANN more or less likely than it already is. The Internet Engineering Task Force, the entirely open process that occupies a crucial role as standard-setter for the Internet, has no tether to the US government yet no one fears its imminent takeover. The regional registries that make policy for Internet protocol address allocations have no contractual or legal tether to the US government, yet no one seems concerned that they will be bulldozed by Chinese or Russian agents. There are no indications that ICANN the corporation, its robust multistakeholder community, or the scores of private corporations and nonprofit organizations who run top level domain registries, want to throw themselves into the hands of the ITU, much less the Russian or Chinese states, simply because the NTIA no longer oversees ICANN.

Keeping ICANN Accountable. The credible risks inherent in the IANA transition come from within ICANN itself. ICANN's status as a California nonprofit with no members cre-

ates a serious accountability deficit, as numerous observers have already pointed out.[16] If ICANN assumes control of both the policy making process and the IANA and Verisign root zone implementation and publishing functions, an ICANN that was taken over by a malevolent faction of its own board, or by its Governmental Advisory Committee, would be very hard to control. Insulated from recall or external accountability, it would have monopoly control of an essential global resource and would be able to leverage that for financial gain and/or forms of Internet regulation inimical to freedom. The real tragedy of the jingoistic Congressional intervention is that has diverted attention from the real issue in the transition: the accountability of ICANN.

Whatever the merits or demerits of U.S. control of ICANN, it did provide an external check on ICANN's behavior. Lurking in the background there was always the threat that serious forms of misbehavior would lead to the withdrawal of the IANA contract. Once the NTIA is no longer the principal and ICANN no longer the agent, what form of external accountability will replace it? Unfortunately, ICANN itself has tried to avoid coming to grips with this question. It has blithely assumed that the purpose of the IANA transition is simply to transfer control of the IANA to itself.

One of the key principles that should guide the transition is to structurally separate root zone file modification (the IANA functions) from policymaking. Structural separation eliminates the concentration of too much power in one organization's hands and has good transparency features. One of the unfortunate legacies of U.S. control of the root zone is that many people now view root zone management as a site for public oversight and policy intervention, a point of leverage for control. This is a mistake. The IANA function should be a technical collective consensus. Final implementation of root zone changes authorized by policy should not be a way for governments (or anyone else) to alter, override or block policy decisions made by the multi-stakeholder process. Nor should control of the root zone be used as leverage for non-DNS related

The nationalistic reaction is a classic example of why the state — any state — is inherently incapable of getting global Internet governance right.

implementation role. Its purpose is to ensure that all top level domain names are globally unique; that all technical data in the root zone file correctly maps each domain to the right nameserver IP addresses; and that legitimate requests for changes, additions or deletions in the root are accurately and securely executed.

Implementation decisions are completely different from policy development. Policy determines which top-level domain names are acceptable, how many there should be, how they are run, etc. Policy development should take place within ICANN's open process, where all stakeholders can be represented in a balanced manner and there is a well-defined process for reaching

foreign policy or economic objectives. This implies that the IANA functions should be organizationally separated from ICANN itself. A solution that separates IANA from ICANN would also be harder for any renegade faction to take over or capture.

A detailed blueprint for the IANA transition is outside the scope of this article. But several proposals have been made elsewhere.[17] It will be interesting to see whether the global multi-stakeholder community invoked by the Commerce Department will be able to come to an agreement on a specific plan. If they can, ICANN will once again be at the forefront of institutional innovations in global governance.

NOTES

1 IANA stands for the Internet Assigned Numbers Authority. The current IANA functions contract is posted here: http://www.ntia.doc.gov/page/iana-functions-purchase-order

2 See Brian Kahin & J. H. Keller (eds.), Coordinating the Internet. (Cambridge, Mass.: MIT Press, 1997).

3 Clinton, William J., and Albert Gore. "Framework for Global Electronic Commerce." Washington, DC: The White House, 1997.

4 NTIA. "Statement of Policy on the Management of Internet Names and Addresses." U.S. Department of Commerce. Washington, DC, June 5, 1998. Retrieved from http://www.ntia.doc.gov/federal-register-notice/1998/statement-policy-management-internet-names-and-addresses

5 Verisign, the world's largest commercial TLD registry, operates .com, .net and other top level domains. Its Cooperative Agreement dates back to 1991, when its predecessor won a NSF bid to operate the name and address registry. Amendment 11 of the agreement (October 1998) requires Verisign to implement only those changes in the root zone file that NTIA approves.

6 Declaration of the Independent Review Panel, INTERNATIONAL CENTRE FOR DISPUTE RESOLUTION ICDR Case No. 50 117 T 00224 08. https://www.icann.org/en/system/files/files/-panel-declaration-19feb10-en.pdf

7 Kevin McGillivray, "Give It Away Now? Renewal of the Iana Functions Contract and Its Role in Internet Governance." International Journal of Law and Information Technology (January 2014): 1-24. http://ijlit.oxfordjournals.org/content/early/2014/01/08/ijlit.eat017.short?rss=1

8 Department of Homeland Security. "Information Technology Sector Risk Management Strategy for the Provide Domain Name Resolution Services Critical Function," Washington DC: Department of Homeland Security, 2011. http://www.dhs.gov/xlibrary/assets/it-sector-risk-management-strategy-domain-name-resolution-services-june2011.pdf

9 Mueller, Milton L. Networks and States: The Global Politics of Internet Governance. (Cambridge, MA: MIT Press, 2010), Chapter 5.

10 Richard Hill, The New International Telecommunications Regulations and the Internet: A Commentary and Legislative History. (Berlin: Springer, 2014); Laura DeNardis, The Global War for Internet Governance, (New Haven: Yale University Press, 2014).

11 Jonathan Weinberg, "Governments, Privatization, and "Privatization": ICANN and the GAC," Michigan Telecommunications & Technology Law Review 18:1, 189-218 (2011), http://www.mttlr.org/voleighteen/weinberg.pdf

12 NTIA, U.S. Principles on the Internet's Domain Name and Addressing System, June 30, 2005. http://www.ntia.doc.gov/other-publication/2005/us-principles-internets-domain-name-and-addressing-system. Note that in June 2005, the U.S.'s "historic" role in authorizing changes or modifications to the DNS root was just over 6 years old.

13 The Montevideo Statement. October 7, 2013. https://www.icann.org/news/announcement-2013-10-07-en

14 NTIA Announces Intent to Transition Key Internet Domain Name Functions. NTIA, Office of Public Affairs, March 14, 2014. http://www.ntia.doc.gov/press-release/2014/ntia-announces-intent-transition-key-internet-domain-name-functions

15 Robert Romano, "Giving away the Internet surrenders the First Amendment," NetRight Daily, 20 March, 2014. http://netrightdaily.com/2014/03/giving-away-internet-surrenders-first-amendment/#ixzz33EMriIeu

16 Milton L. Mueller, "ICANN, Inc.: Accountability and Participation in the Governance of Critical Internet Resources." Korean Journal of Policy Studies 24:2 (2009): 91-116; Thomas Lenard and Lawrence White, Lawrence. (2009). ICANN at a Crossroads: A Proposal for Better Governance and Performance. Washington, DC: Technology Policy Institute (March). http://www.techpolicyinstitute.org/files/icann%20at%20a%20crossroads1.pdf; Rolf H. Weber and R. Shawn Gunnarson, "A Constitutional Solution for Internet Governance," Columbia Science and Technology Law Review 14 (Fall 2012). Available at SSRN: http://ssrn.com/abstract=2076780; See also Internet Governance Project blog, "ICANN's Accountability Meltdown: A 4-part series" (August – September 2013). Retrieved from http://www.internetgovernance.org/2013/08/31/icanns-accountability-meltdown-a-four-part-series/ http://www.internetgovernance.org/2013/09/05/meltdown-ii-the-unilateral-right-to-amend/ http://www.internetgovernance.org/2013/09/14/meltdown-iii-how-top-down-implementation-replaced-bottom-up-policymaking/ and http://www.internetgovernance.org/2013/09/18/meltdown-iv-how-icann-resists-accountability/

17 Milton L. Mueller and Brenden Kuerbis, "Roadmap for globalizing IANA: Four principles and a proposal for reform," Internet Governance Project blog, March 3, 2014. http://www.internetgovernance.org/pdf/ICANNreformglobalizingIANAfinal.pdf

Cyberdefense

The Worst of All Cyber Construction Sites

Sandro Gaycken

Most people expect militaries to be of outstanding quality when it comes to security. Usually, they are right. Militaries work under a tight set of security-driven conditions and the consequences of failure are of utmost severity – the loss of life, power, wealth, and independence. These failures occur on a significantly larger scale than in any comparable context, which is why most countries place a heavy emphasis on defense.

However, the focus on defense is constantly shifting, according to political and strategic changes and due to tradeoffs usually associated with high military costs. In peacetime, militaries with little to no troops in any theater facing a low risk of a larger military conflict at home will be under economic and political scrutiny. The current rationale among Europeans right now is that a military should only maintain a rudimentary set of capabilities which can be quickly expanded should a conflict ever begin to emerge, assisted by the pooling and sharing of resources in any other circumstances.[1]

Militaries lament this sentiment, but given the extreme unlikeliness of an all-out war in core Europe and its more tangible economic troubles, scrutiny of the military is justi-

Sandro Gaycken is a senior researcher at the Department of Computer Science, Freie Universität Berlin, Germany, focusing on cyberwar and cyberespionage. He is an EastWest senior fellow, a fellow at Oxford University's Martin School, a fellow of the German Council on Foreign Relations, a project director in the NATO SPS Program on cyberdefense and cyberstrategy, a former cybersecurity strategist of the German Federal Foreign Office, a regular cybersecurity adviser for the German Bundestag, and an expert witness for legal cases on military cyberespionage.

fied. There may be arguments to the contrary, of course, but overly voluminous military apparatuses are probably not necessary at this time.

After they calm down, militaries react in three ways to an economic downgrade. They technologize more to convert higher personnel costs into lower acquisition and maintenance costs, they strongly prioritize their capabilities into "what is really needed" and what is probably less of a concern, and they justify their actions more and try to behave more fiscally responsible. For cybersecurity, all of this is bad.

(1) The higher technologization extends in two directions: quality and quantity. Better technology — with higher capabilities for fewer personnel — and more technology are supposed to assure capabilities even with dwindling funds and forces. Computers turned out to be the foundation for this kind of progress. This paradigm became explicitly known as "smart defense".[2] Better technology was usually achieved through computerized gadgets and centralization through IT. And more technology, accordingly, resulted in a lot of these computers everywhere.

(2) The prioritization is mainly tactical and political. Most militaries informationalized extensively only after the Cold War, where the military climate was no longer determined by large-scale interstate warfare and highly efficient espionage and sabotage, but by guerilla warfare. Consequently, the tactical-technological emphasis in innovation shifted to mobility, reconnaissance, high-speed communication and situational awareness among different kinds of troops and allies and away from counterintelligence and strong operational security and robustness. This led to the "network-centric" paradigm, which necessitates complex IT-networks at its core to function.[3]

(3) The stronger need for justification and economization of military programs reduced the margin of error considered acceptable in acquisition and development decision-making and enforced the prioritization of economic solutions, except for some areas considered highly important, such as air power.[4]

All three problems finally merged in an awful set of security-hostility specifications and conditions for military IT. As a result, connectivity, standardization, centralization, commercial feasibility and compatibility with a standard-IT-educated workforce were main drivers of the military for decades. IT-security wasn't considered an outright necessity, given the low-tech character of the guerilla forces in question and the mild overall dependence on IT. In addition, an unspecialized workforce with a standard IT-background was in charge of technology acquisition, and preferred cheap technologies while failing to rectify anything they probably did wrong in the process.

This combination and hierarchy of specifications led to the widespread adoption of Commercial-Off-The-Shelf (COTS) IT, implemented according to guerilla-tactics and economic and IT-inherent innovation paradigms, and developed and maintained by a standard IT workforce and business data processing specialists.

This has created a list of highly critical and persistent problems for military cyberdefense.

A core concern is high basic vulnerabilities. Every part of a COTS-IT has tens of thousands of critical vulnerabilities, most of which can be used as single points of failure for any system or process attached to it, given an attack by a knowledgeable adversary.[5] In addition, COTS-IT is produced, delivered and frequently maintained in insecure environments.[6]

Another issue is complexity. Present systems, networks (closed or open) and processes are far too complex and too interwoven to attain in-depth knowledge of the whole system, all its possible processes and all potential consequences.[7] Illegitimate activity can hide in the noise of data, camouflaged as legitimate processes, so even Big Data analyses can be fooled. Knowledgeable attackers can hide perfectly inside these systems for years. IT-security is also a complex task, and further complicated by the enormous size of its systemic connections to multiple military processes. The military's high demand is often met only by a moderately competent workforce in acquisition, design and operation, which is largely in rotation and organized inefficiently.[8]

The IT-security industry is another problem. Some industry salesmen and researchers want to capitalize on IT-insecurity, despite their incompetence in security or their failure to understand military demands or specifications. Consequently, they sell immature and insecure concepts and products on top of the COTS-legacy, reinforc-ing malicious old path dependencies instead of questioning them.[9]

These are just some of the core problems – many more could be added. As a result, the state of affairs in most high-tech militaries is difficult and insecure.

A single, well-prepared insider from an entire military workforce could infiltrate a whole system.

A single, well-prepared insider from an entire military workforce could infiltrate a whole system. Most infiltrations will be critical and can exploit multiple systemic single points of failure. It is highly unlikely that any infiltrator will ever be detected; exploits can lie dormant for years. It's neither complicated nor expensive to produce and introduce such attacks. And since Stuxnet and Snowden, more and more offensive actors are interested and able to execute such operations.

The strategic end result is theoretically highly interesting. Thermonuclear warfare (nuclear weapons are not yet extensively connected), completely low-tech warfare, and high-tech warfare against purely low-tech guerillas are still possible, but any other kind of conflict will soon be obsolete. This renders a larger part of our military technology into expensive scrap metal.

Snowden to the Rescue. While people may expect militaries to possess outstanding cyberdefense this is not the case. Some military systems even deteriorate further by implementing ever more vulnerable IT. A recent idea among some militaries in Europe is to utilize standard Enterprise Resource

Planning (ERP) business software for command and control, which is known to inherit hundreds of thousands of vulnerabilities.[10]

But there was a change: Snowden came to the rescue. Before him, most militaries chided the above concerns as unsubstantiated doom-mongering and dismissed demands for more substantial reforms as "unrealistic". Now, however, the excessive and systemic failure of conventional IT and IT-security when confronted with a professional intelligence service is documented and less deniable.[11] Given this proof of interests, capabilities and weaknesses, the previous perception of "reality" has taken a 180-degree turn. Systemic dependencies upon entirely uncontrollable, vulnerable and accessible systems are beginning to appear a little more unrealistic than spending more money and effort on IT.

However, the direction of this change is not entirely clear. Something has to happen. But what? And where? And who should do it? These answers are far from clear and not easy to provide.

Dark Matters.
A main cause for the difficulty to provide definite answers in cybersecurity at large and military cyberdefense in particular is the bad visibility of incidents combined with the complicatedness of the field.

Bad visibility is a long-known problem.[12] A lot of dark fields must be expected as the complexity of the systems allows a lot of invisible and undetectable activities. But this is a guess with only anecdotal evidence to substantiate it, such as the alleged number of U.S. Cyber Command operations in 2011 according to leaked documents (231), in comparison to the number of operations detected during that year (1).[13] Also, many dark fields intersect in "superdark" fields, where threats, numbers, damages and security efficiencies are equally unknown. This is a classical realm of cyber tales and mythos, where both nothing and everything can happen.

Extrapolating flashlight incidents into larger pictures would be an option to get a better view, but here, complexity steps in. Extrapolation would require incident-oriented, near-complete in-depth testing to realize basic vulnerabilities, which in turn would have to be mapped to detailed intelligence about foreign offensive capabilities of appropriate potential adversaries and checked systematically against strategic scenarios. However, systemic in-depth testing is not conceptualized very well and completeness of testing seems impossible as the number of attack vectors and tactics is either finite and non-denumerable or even infinite.[14] Intelligence about foreign capabilities is still not mature, the history of offensive cyber capabilities is still young, and existing lists of strategic scenarios are underdeveloped and too conservative.[15]

An important adjacent problem is how to assess security in this case. Current concepts of cybersecurity must be considered incomplete. The focus has always been too technical and limited on the idea of a perimeter with access nodes.[16] No one really knows how to reliably measure the efficiency of cybersecurity in light of promised functions or of total security. Solid, scientific methods are still missing, and many IT-security companies do not want them because they are uncertain if they will like the results.[17]

The many uncertainties render decision-making and reasoning difficult and demanding, even for experts. For many militaries, this results in

tolerant towards false solutions and not too critical of internal processes, failing to expose militaries to oversight and denying protection through affirmative external opinion. The "good

A climate of fear and indecision has been an immediate result, accompanied by unnecessarily high confidentiality, as secrecy seemed a more immediately feasible measure to protect against potential threats.

an uncomfortable situation. Military personnel mostly lack particular specialties, and salespeople and experts tell them broadly varying stories about possible solutions. A lot of proposed solutions are highly expensive, political pressure is high, and — as has been illustrated above — economic and public scrutiny do not tolerate or forgive wrong and expensive decisions.

A climate of fear and indecision has been an immediate result, accompanied by unnecessarily high confidentiality, as secrecy seemed a more immediately feasible measure to protect against potential threats — and as it generated some protection from scrutiny in passing.

Bad Ideas. In short time, a few unhealthy paradigms for acquisition and innovation evolved, which appear every now and then to varying extent.

The "big fish" strategy is very popular. IT is acquired, developed and maintained by the biggest vendors, as they seem the most competent, and relegating decisions to such actors seems in itself competent. In the "friendly partner" strategy, IT is assessed, acquired and developed with partners who are

story" strategy chooses the most intelligible and actionable lobbyist story, best suited to the political and economical views of decision-makers. Friendly partners with good stories led to the prioritization of peripheral approaches with a high acceptance towards basic malicious path dependencies. Another popular strategy is the "OGP (Other Guy's Problem)" strategy. Here, the decision-makers try to disperse, delegate or outsource responsibility. The ideal outcome is not to make any critical decisions at all, but have someone else make them. A part of this strategy is the still prominent excuse to assign most of the blame to the end-user for his/her security incompetence. But this excuse "forgets" that critical technology must always be highly usable, clear, and intelligible for a user. If this precondition is not met, the user can hardly be blamed. And most if not all IT and IT-security is more or less user-hostile. The "got to start somewhere" strategy is a last variant and on the rise. A lot of militaries feel high pressure from politics and other militaries to "do something" about cybersecurity. Many of them simply start with "something" under the double impression that something is better than nothing and that anything that is bought now can still be optimized later. But both assumptions are wrong. False solutions only create new malicious path dependencies. And vendors abuse uncertainties to promise endless possibilities for optimization, while not mentioning (and frequently not knowing or acknowledging) structural deficits and gaps of the security concepts as such.

In many cases, strategies are being combined. Their effect is usually negative. They negatively affect the climate of decision-making, of innovation and — in many cases —security.

Natural Evolution. There is light at the end of the tunnel. Nature is on the side of security. What many militaries have forgotten (strangely, but apparently) is the fact that military capabilities which applies particularly strongly to security. Critical processes and contexts have to be highly secure. Even though this perspective may seem strange for some militaries at present, many other militaries still assume this point of view, as do many companies and researchers, eventually forcing others into it.

As such, this natural mechanism will generate a real security evolution. The more serious actors will eventually remove most uncertainties about insecurity and security, and once those problems are resolved, real and reliable solutions will gain traction and cannot be ignored or contested by other, less-informed or biased actors. The process will reward those with courage and open minds, who strove first for actual solutions. Those actors will likely gain permanent competitive and strategic advantages, as their technology base will be broader and less infested, their

No matter how nice your neighbors are—as long as you don't have your own abilities for security, you can never be certain in your decision-making and you can never be fully at peace.

simply have to be efficient and effective. No matter whether you are a realist or not, simply jeopardizing your capabilities is not an option. The natural law elegantly explained by Hobbes sets in. No matter how nice your neighbors are, how deep your peace is — as long as you don't have your own abilities for security, you can never be certain in your decision-making and you can never be fully at peace. For technology, this creates a transitive natural law, knowledge base will be more thorough and extensive, and they will have more competent people.

Assuming the presence of such a natural law for security and in light of the aforementioned difficulties, the past, present and future development of cyberdefense can be sketched out to some extent. Five phases of varying duration seem plausible.

Phase one was the long phase of the past where security was an afterthought and not considered a significant problem. Solutions, institutions, laws and theories were undifferentiated and conceptualized as "one-size-fits-all". The neglect created it's own legacy. IT-insecurity in combination with critical dependencies and extensive accessibility generated great offensive opportunities, which attracted more and more attackers. The duration of the neglect also manifested certain "security mentalities" in most security actors and producers, predominantly involving the assumption that security will always remain a low, neglected priority with little resources and little tolerance, in turn conditioning these actors to adopt small and discreet perspectives and behaviors.

Phase two is the present phase of the problem. Serious incidents are on the rise, and the continuity of bad news illuminates the presence of structural deficits. Progress starts by multiple differentiations to better master the complexity of the topic and move away from "one-size-fits-all" structures. Theoretical differentiations will generate theoretical distinctions, scientific disciplines, specializations and systematic zoologies of assets, threats, weaknesses and measures. Practical differentiations will create a heterogeneous workforce, a number of different new institutions and responsibilities, new laws and standards, and novel technical approaches. Technical approaches will still largely be "quick fixes", unlikely to offer hard and sustainable security advances. Offense gains more knowledge and understanding as well, but it is not fully established with most actors. While it is clearly on the rise and attracting higher quantities and qualities, the broader establishment of security frustrates and excludes some of the less talented attackers.

Phase three is about to begin. Knowledge and understanding is maturing, and dark fields are illuminated as far as possible. Incidents are understood and strategies are calculable. Intelligence provides useful and extensive information about offenders. Science provides theories and methods. Security efficiency becomes more clear, inasmuch as the need for strategic and informed approaches to cybersecurity. Differentiated expertise, responsibilities and institutions provide effective and in-depth assistance and steering. The present half-blind trial-and-error security tinkering is starting to be replaced by systematic, systemic and holistic security innovation including substantial interaction with or reduction of the IT innovation process at large. Security actors and producers stuck in old IT-security mentalities will be combed out. Implementation has only started and requires more economic and political strategies, so offense is still possible and profitable, but requires more competence and capability if directed towards critical assets.

In phase four, systematic security innovation is a mature process and spans all technologies. Additional external mechanisms are in place and mostly effective. Economic and political strategies are in place to warrant progress and implementation in all relevant contexts. Security maturity is approaching its final stages towards very high resilience. Highly scaling or critical offense is getting tough and is more and more reserved for superpowers. Lesser powers will be frustrated and controllable.

Phase five is the "as-secure-as-it-gets" information society.

Wise Progress.

Other analysts may have different views on the future of the security problem, but given the natural laws of security and offense, the complexity of the problem, its current outset, the unbelievable extent of baseline insecurity, and the deep path dependencies as strong conditions and dynamics, this seems like a plausible development.

If it is true to some extent, the current phase of general enlightenment and theoretical and pragmatic differentiation can be modeled and assisted to formulate a desirable outcome, and some preparations can be taken for upcoming phases to enable an efficient, swift, value-sensitive, and profitable transgression.

An overarching aim should be a model and the achievement of "wise progress" in this field. The term "wise" may sound strange and somewhat less effective than the commonly used term, "smart". But the present approaches to "smart x" are not exactly awe-inspiring. The basic paradigm of smart progress seems to be to collect all sorts of expensive components or people, glue them together somehow, and hope that the outcome is better than before. Wisdom is different. Wisdom is to know the exact needs of something and applying an ideal solution for this exact and actual need. Accordingly, "wise progress" would first find out exactly what the problem is and take its time to design the right solution.

Some first ideas can be given to facilitate such wise progress during the next phases in military and general cybersecurity development:

- Model evolutions: By acknowledging and understanding the natural laws of security and offense, the inherent laws of technological innovation and accompanying laws and rules about market and policy dynamics, different kinds of evolutions can be predicted for particular actors, motivations, techniques, institutions and similar entities, in addition to side-effects, net-effects and evolutionary competition. Such an evolutionary modeling would enable the prediction of certain stages of security maturity and allow wise interference and interlocking of other evolutions.

- Pick your fights: An important part of this evolutionary modeling is the prohibition of own or foreign evolutions, which may be too early or detrimental to security or other values. In particular, actors should not initiate arms races they cannot win in the long term. An example is the general emergence of cyberwarfare, to which the industrialized West (who delivered the precedence) is much more vulnerable than its rivals. Another more concrete example could be sensors, forensics and big data analytics . Attackers' counterevolution in spoofing, false flag operations or hiding has not been predicted, but may very well be highly efficient and escalatory across all current security approaches, leading to a dangerous overall decrease in security. Protection of the security mechanisms themselves is underinvestigated as well.[19]

- Shape competences: If it becomes perceivable that new approaches are required, one can start to create basic competences for the next phases. This will prepare and catalyze change. Experts and specialists should be educated, but should be "open minded" and not be taught deficient security mentalities. Coupled with evolutionary predictions of cybersecurity, the shaping of competence is a powerful overall catalyzer of certain variants of change.

•Pause questionable progress: Spending a lot of money to develop and implement IT for critical contexts may be a bad decision at the moment, as specifications for such IT may change dramatically over the next months and years. It may be wiser to spare money and wait for things to develop or to spend those resources on IT-security (or at least some of those resources on a prediction of the development of the overall IT-security situation).

•Prepare (for) migrations: Once convinced of the necessity of change, economic and political strategies for migrations from insecure to secure systems for critical application contexts will be among the most helpful supportive measures to assure a quick, correct and beneficial security reform.[20]

Many more supportive measures are conceivable to catalyze, shape and control the up-and-coming necessary progress in cybersecurity. Wise and open perspectives and approaches to this phenomenon will help understand, determine and realize the progress we actually want.

NOTES

1 See Jamie Shea, *NATO post-2014 - Preserving the Essentials*, in: Biscop, Sven & Fiott, Daniel, „The State of Defence in Europe — State of Emergency", Egmont Paper 62, Brussels 2013; and: Jo Coelmont & Alexander Mattelaer, *Capability Development — The Time They Are A-Changing*, in: Biscop, Sven & Fiott, Daniel, „The State of Defence in Europe — State of Emergency", Egmont Paper 62, Brussels 2013.

2 Henius, Jakob, &Jacopo Leone McDonald. *Smart Defense: A Critical Appraisal*. NATO defense College, Research division= Collège de défense de l'Otan, Division recherche, 2012.

3 Persson, Mats, and Georgios Rigas. "Complexity: the dark side of network-centric warfare." *Cognition, technology & work* 16.1 (2014): 103-115.

4 Hensel, Nayantara. *The Impact of Economic Austerity on US and European Defense Industrial Bases*. No. NPS-AM-11-C8P11R02-046. DEPARTMENT OF THE NAVY WASHINGTON DC, 2011.

5 http://www.coverity.com/press-releases/annual-coverity-scan-report-finds-open-source-and-proprietary-software-quality-better-than-industry-average-for-second-consecutive-year/

6 http://www.dailytech.com/US+GOA+40+Percent+of+Defense+Supply+Chain+Damaged+by+Chinese+Parts/article21937.htm

7 Liu, Jin-Xing, Shao-Dong Chen, and Yan-Gao Wang. "Study on node importance of complex network based military Command Control networks.", see above

8 Bodden, Eric, et al. "Reducing human factors in software security architectures." *Future Security Conference (to appear)*. 2013.

9 http://www.washingtonpost.com/business/capitalbusiness/lobbying-on-data-cybersecurity-has-tripled/2014/05/11/fad0fe12-d6e9-11e3-8a78-8fe50322a72c_story.html

10 https://www.virtualforge.com/en/labs/benchmark.html

11 See especially: http://en.wikipedia.org/wiki/NSA_ANT_catalog

12 http://www.darkreading.com/risk/the-problem-with-cyber-insurance/a/d-id/1269682; see also: Böhme, Rainer, and Tyler Moore. "Security Metrics and Security Investment.", online at: http://lyle.smu.edu/~tylerm/courses/econsec/reading/lnse-secinv2.pdf (accessed 30th June 2014).

13 http://www.washingtonpost.com/world/national-security/us-spy-agencies-mounted-231-offensive-cyber-operations-in-2011-documents-show/2013/08/30/d090a6ae-119e-11e3-b4cb-fd7ce041d814_story.html

14 For Turing machines, Turing's halting problem or its many-to-one reduction in Rice's theorem suggest as much.

15 Sandro Gaycken, *Cyberwar—Das Internet als Kriegsschauplatz*, Open Source Press, Munich 2010; and Sandro Gaycken, *Cyberwar Einführung*,Introductory Teaching Material on Strategic Cyberwar, free and online at: http://www.inf.fu-berlin.de/groups/ag-si/pub/Cyberwar_SB1-5_V160114.pdf

16 Dave McMahon, *Beyond Perimeter Defense*, in: Melissa Hathaway, „Best Practices in Computer Network Defense", NATO SPS Series, D: Information and Communication Security — Vol 35, Brussel 2014

17 See: Sandro Gaycken, *Statement for NSA Commission of the German Bundestag*, June 2014, online at: http://www.bundestag.de/blob/285124/7115462c38da14ffa77b68489318253f/mat_a_sv-1-1-pdf-data.pdf; and similar: Michael Waidner, *Statement for NSA Commission of the German Bundestag*, June 2014, online at: http://www.bundestag.de/blob/285122/2f815a7598a9a7e9b4162d70173ecedb/mat_a_sv-1-2-pdf-data.pdf, both accessed 30th June 2014

18 Bhatti, Rafae, et al. "Emerging trends around big data analytics and security: panel." *Proceedings of the 17th ACM symposium on Access Control Models and Technologies*. ACM, 2012.

19 Schell, Roger. "Security—A big question for big data." *Big Data, 2013 IEEE International Conference on*. IEEE, 2013.

20 A project to research some first factors and options is currently in preparation.

Safety&Security

Taking Control of Our Cyber Future

Melissa E. Hathaway and John N. Stewart

Despite efforts by experienced and driven professionals, multiple cybersecurity challenges plague us today. Key indicators suggest that we are not making enough progress and, in fact, are possibly going backwards. Organizations of all types, including companies, governments, schools, and critical infrastructures, are experiencing increased data breaches, criminal activity, essential e-services disruption, and property destruction.[1]

This must change.

To make differences at scale, this paper outlines four actions, from two points of view: a view focused towards technology and practice, and a view towards policy and law.

The four actions proposed are:
- Connected devices need minimum standards and enforcement;
- Security practice must return to the basics;
- The market needs additional influence; and
- Executive accountability for cyber is required.

The paper discusses these actions and additional solutions to each, with associated key performance indicators (KPIs). These effectiveness and performance indicators should help decision makers take action and monitor their progress and

Melissa E. Hathaway is President of Hathaway Global Strategies, LLC and a Senior Advisor at Harvard Kennedy School's Belfer Center for Science and International Affairs. In addition to spearheading the national cybersecurity agendas for both President George W. Bush and President Obama, she is a Distinguished Fellow at the Centre for International Governance Innovation in Canada, the Chair of the Council of Experts for the Global Cyber Security Center in Italy, and serves on the Board of Regents at Potomac Institute for Policy Studies.

John N. Stewart is the Senior Vice President and Chief Security Officer at Cisco Systems, Inc. For 25 years, he has led or participated in security initiatives ranging from elementary school information technology design to national security programs. In addition to sitting on various technical advisory boards, he is on the Board of Directors for Shadow Networks, Inc. and the National Cyber-Forensics Training Alliance (NCFTA). He also serves on the Cybersecurity Think Tank at University of Maryland University College.

success, should they adopt this advice.

Background and Observations.

Consumers, companies, and nations are all at risk, and data indicates the different types of risks are growing.

The first risk is a breach. The number of breached records rose by 350 percent in 2013, with approximately half of the U.S. population's personal information exposed in a 12-month period.[2, 3] The average time it takes an organization to detect a breach is 32 days, an increase of 55 percent from last year.[4] Most organizations experience two *successful* breaches per week where their core networks or enterprise system is infiltrated.[5]

The second risk is crime and financial, informational, and industrial espionage. By one estimate, cybercrime and economic espionage costs an estimated 445 billion U.S. dollars globally (this is an increase from last year).[6] Theft of Intellectual Property (IP) in the United States is calculated as a loss to the tune of hundreds of billions of dollars.[7] Organizations are increas-

The third risk is disruption of e-services. For example, a Distributed Denial of Service (DDoS) campaign has been underway for the last year against the United States' top financial institutions, including JPMorgan Chase, Bank of America, Citigroup, U.S. Bank, and PNC. The DDoS attacks are reaching levels that are disrupting citizens' ability to conduct banking, and telecommunications providers can no longer guarantee quality of service or business continuity.[10]

The final risk is destruction. In August 2012, Saudi Aramco suffered a targeted attack that used malicious software to destroy data and damaged nearly 75 percent of the company's IT infrastructure. Corporate officials declared it a targeted attack intended to affect oil production.[11] A few months later, in March 2013, multiple financial institutions in South Korea, including Shinhan Bank—the country's fourth largest bank—suffered damages from malware similar to that used in the incident against Saudi Aramco. Their e-services were disrupted and data was

Most organizations experience two *successful* breaches per week where their core networks or enterprise system is infiltrated.

ing their operational expenditures to defend themselves from and attend to security issues caused by malicious software and pirated software.[8] According to the IDC's 2014 estimate, the global total for losses to enterprises will approach half a trillion dollars and continue climbing for 2014.[9]

destroyed.

Cyber breaches, crime, disruption, and destruction have significant implications for global trade and global business continuity. It is time to change course, and propose implementable solutions.

Connected Devices Need Minimum Standards and Enforcement.

When a true story is printed explaining how refrigerators were used to generate SPAM emails, it is both a humorous story and an alarming indicator.[12]

Today, there are no standards—much less enforceable ones—for devices connecting to the Internet, aside from those inconsistently created by network operators. In addition, entire industries are now building connectable devices with little to no experience or history in building (secure, resilient, well-engineered) connectable devices. This combination of poor product testing and vendor inexperience is resulting in baby-monitors, cameras, and cars being exploitable.[13]

We face a crossroad. First, traditional systems such as PC's, tablets, and smart phones already constitute a very significant cybersecurity challenge, as the data shows. Second, we have the addition of the Internet of Things (IoT) - defined here as all network/Internet-connected devices *not* including PCs, tablets, and smart phones. In 2014, it is estimated that an additional 6.8 billion IoT devices will be produced.[14] Both traditional and IoT devices have similar security requirements, albeit the IoT devices include both known and unknown vendors in the IT space, have different power, memory and CPU limitations, and are quickly redefining how much human traffic versus Machine to Machine (M2M) exists as a percentage of total network traffic.

Each traditional and IoT system has the components necessary to be a security threat. They have:

- A network interface;
- Software; and
- A person who will seek to use the system in some way other than intended.

IoT devices are increasingly produced by known brands that did not grow up as IT companies (e.g., Samsung, Toyota, Epson, LG, Bosch, Coca-Cola, etc.). These next-generation devices will now have some or many network connections: Ethernet, wireless (cellular, 802.11x, ZigBee), Bluetooth, or proprietary wireless. These devices will be vulnerable, unable to have built in security protections sufficient to the task, if any at all.[15]

Additionally, these previously standalone devices will now run software that uses a network or networks for some purpose and probably will not be built with a security development lifecycle and review. Most large companies (e.g., Cisco, Microsoft, Oracle, etc.) that have produced Internet-connected systems to date have always had, or at least have now, a Security Development Lifecycle.[16] This assists in market differentiation, reduces flaws in fielded products, and assists in product certifications.[17] These new entrants are soon to discover how vulnerabilities in software will change their market. Unfortunately, society will also learn how these flaws change and challenge safety, resiliency, and personal privacy.

By 2020—just six years from now—over 20 billion devices will be connected to the Internet and the number of connected people will at least double, which represents half the world's projected population.[18, 19] How many new vendors will join the future Internet with their products? How many products will be innovated and built with security in mind in that same six-year period?

Proposed Solution(s). *Underwriters Laboratory for Connected Devices.*[20]

In 1894, William Henry Merrill created the Underwriters Laboratory (UL) in Northbrook, Illinois. The electrical industry at the time suffered problems. Electricity could be dangerous, as poorly designed systems affected the power grid of the time, and needed both standards and testing labs for adherences. Today, UL is a worldwide operation addressing seven business areas, and ensuring, with its stamp of approval, that consumers are knowledgeable and testing is done.

In 2014, the Internet faces a similar problem. Anyone can build an Internet-connectable device, there are no standards, and these devices can in turn affect other devices on the Internet. There is no lab or certification process for Internet-connected devices to determine their readiness or level of security, nor any stamp of approval suggesting they were tested.

The creation of an Internet Underwriters Laboratory (IUL), which tests and has the manufacturer test their products against cybersecurity requirements, would assure a fault-tolerant range of some size. This, however, cannot be done independent of the insurance industry, as we learned from UL's history.[21] Motivated by self-interest, the insurance companies helped create UL to lower the risk as products and services were created, so as to lower the cost of the insurance paid to compensate if this risk were to occur. Key to this process was the common interest that both insurance companies and consumers had to provide transparency on what the risk factors were to accurately account for the "cost" of the insurance.[22] Today, we do not have models to get at that type of data, as devices and systems are too often built without risk and mitigation in mind, and then not tested to verify efficacy.

An important second-order effect would be reviews and comparisons of products and services. These comparisons would be based on reporting and results from the testing, and could lead to a "Consumer Reports"-like initiative with independence and impartiality. This helps change markets, as it would ensure that the buyer understands how the products were built, and if the next refrigerator, baby monitor, or other connected device represents a lower threat for the environment, be it a business or a home.

In 1915, UL was issuing 50 million labels per year to be attached to certified products. By 1922, it was 50 million labels per month.[23] A similar adoption rate should be possible in a "Connected Devices" IUL and, if created, this would be a key indicator of progress. In addition, existing industries would benefit from the testing data/empirical data (cyber insurance) to inform their future product and service lines of business. New industries (market entrants) could drive innovation using the testing results (consumer reports) to produce new products and services—displacing those that are less safe, secure, and resilient.

Internet Service Providers— Upstream Security for Downstream Devices. The market for

connected devices is growing quickly, as is the number of connected devices. This is enabled by some combination of low cost computing and data storage; inexpensive, portable consumer devices; and high-speed bandwidth that allows you to click, connect, and search data or provision e-services 24 hours a day, seven days a week. More and more people bring-their-own-device (BYOD) to work or school and third party data storage or hosting facilities allow for low-latency access to that data globally. More and more organizations are installing IP cameras for protection, automated machinery that is IP connected, or building control software for heating and cooling. Even if we can get the devices to be more securely designed, tested, and provisioned, we should at the same time consider additional solutions in the network.

Connected devices require Internet connectivity and that is most-often provisioned through a single set of vendors—the Internet Service Providers (ISPs). ISPs come in many forms and sizes and go by many names: the phone company, the cable company, the wireless company, etc. Yet when you look at who is responsible for provisioning this access, you find that approximately twenty-five ISPs carry as much as 80 percent of all Internet traffic.[24] That is a small number of organizations that could make a difference at scale.

ISPs have unparalleled access to global networks, giving them a unique view on network traffic. This enables them, with the proper tools and authorities, to detect cyber intrusions and attacks as they are forming and transiting towards their targets.[25] The bulk of Internet pollution (such as SPAM or DDoS attacks) could be stopped before it arrives at its destination using network traffic analysis and core and distributed control points. For example, some ISPs limit SPAM and partner with law enforcement to deny the distribution of child pornography.[26]

ISPs, using more advanced technologies, could also stop a portion of malicious activity before it reaches an organization by invoking upstream security controls deployed at key choke points within the Internet traffic flows (established by an ISP). Bell Canada and CenturyLink are using these types of technologies to provide a safer Internet experience for their customers, and have proven that this type of service reduces overall corporate costs by reducing the rate of infections to its customers.[27] As connected devices become infected with malicious software, ISPs could see that too if alerted that a device or entity is using excessive bandwidth, is trying to further spread the malicious software, or is communicating with a known command server.

ISPs in Europe, Australia, Japan, and even some in the United States have already assumed the duty to inform their customers when machines or devices appear to be participating in a botnet infection.[28] They assist consumers and businesses in isolating the infected devices and, at the same time, work to eliminate or eradicate the infection.

We can no longer be one click away from an infection or worse yet, no service. Therefore, it is time to turn to the ISPs to provide upstream security for our downstream devices. Meeting tomorrow's demands for network capacity, new applications, and an expanding base of users requires anticipating the next-generation security demands today. The ISPs can and should be a central component of the solution.

Security Practice Must Return to the Basics.

Common practice focuses on the protection of the physical asset and logical function of its components rather than the product or service that it is providing. We need to start focusing on critical services, not critical infrastructures, because it will likely change our views and investments regarding protection, resilience, recovery, and restoration of assets. It may also highlight the interdependencies among organizations and nations requiring different approaches to common defense and security.[29]

A major transition in the IT industry is the notion that servers, storage, where the end consumer of that service is either denied access to the service, or the service is interdicted and so is delivered differently than expected. These are "new" threats: where what you think you are doing and the information you are getting is *not the actual service or the information because it has been manipulated*. Examples include malware in the browser (MITB) that manipulates bank web site surfing; a government creating a false website to lure foreign citizens into providing information or using a government intercepted communications service, or a fake wireless access point to lure visitors and steal personal information.[30, 31]

Proposed Solution(s).

We need to start talking about everything in security terms, so that resiliency and integrity

We need to start focusing on critical services, not critical infrastructures, because it will likely change our views and investments regarding protection, resilience, recovery, and restoration of assets.

and applications are not at all where IT builds value. It is in the identification, development (in some cases), and operations of the critical services that IT is so much more relevant. For example, the fact that an online map site has servers, storage, and applications is not the value added per se — it is the map, directions, visualization, and secondary information that generate value for the consumer.

Part and parcel in today's day and age is where the service can be affected, and may be best addressed. A proper mapping for critical services would include:

- Service's name and purpose;
- The critical functions that are dependent upon that service;
- Each infrastructure element needed to deliver the service, some of which may not be operated by the corporation (e.g., the Internet being part of the way banks deliver service to their customers, although they do not control it);
- The requirements for resiliency

of the service; and

•Continuous Independent Verification and Validation (IV&V), where possible.

Reduce the Threat Surface on Today's Systems.[32]

The hard work is rarely the most fun, and when talking about reducing risk, these words are highly applicable. In Germany, studies show that the average citizen is using over seventy applications from over two dozen vendors, and nearly one out of every seven people in Germany are using Operating Systems (OSs) that are not fully patched, with at least one out of every fifteen applications also not being fully patched.[33] This yields, for just that country, a significant amount of risk due to poorly maintained systems. Germany is by no means alone in this; poorly maintained systems are a global issue.

This data and others show that we are not taking proper care of the basics—patching, upgrading, and testing—and are leaving organizations and people vulnerable as a result. The Top Twenty Critical Security Controls provide an easy checklist of the basic activities that ought to be done and have proven effective in increasing an overall defensive posture.[34] Most penetrations occur against the top eight controls, suggesting that reducing the threat surface in today's systems is possible if the eight controls are applied consistently.

"Back to basics" includes more than just patching. It also includes eliminating "dark space"—the areas where something about a system or a service is not known and needs to be in order to assure its proper operations. An example of dark space is "unknown devices," such as a personally owned computer or unregistered data center system that is connected to a network where no one "knows" what the device is, what it does, or to whom it is related. A second dark space example is "unknown connections," where an Internet or intra-network connection exists and is also unseen, creating an unmanaged side door to a datacenter, corporate network, or production service. Due to their unseen, unknown nature, these dark spaces provide a safe haven for illicit and illegal activity, and thus posit additional risk and fragility. Absent preventative measures, dark space is likely to only be discovered post-breach or post-failure.

The Market Needs Additional Influence.

Many governments have determined that normal market forces are insufficient for the development of effective cybersecurity. Therefore, governments are increasing their market interventions, primarily through regulation and law. In Europe and the United States, this takes the form of defining protection requirements and demanding certain sectors to identify, assess, and correct deficiencies. These sectors include: electric utilities, financial services, transportation, and telecommunications. Other regulatory measures include mandating notification regarding breaches, the technique or method used, and outages or business disruptions (telecommunications), as well as imposing strict data protection controls.[35] Non-compliance may result in penalties, including financial ones. For example, in the United Kingdom, a breach could cost an organization £500,000 if the corporation did not have proper defenses in place.[36] These types of penalties get the attention of corporate leaders. Yet at the same time, if the necessary security preventative measures are costly, organizations may delay implementing them, quietly reflecting: "It will not happen to me."

These interventions introduce new issues because data protection is often handled by a different part of the government than information security. Well-meaning government officials do not always consider how a new policy, sometimes localized by country or region, could conflict with other existing policies. In Europe, for example, data protection directives impose strict controls on protecting personally-identifiable information. This directly conflicts with the draft Directive on Network and Information Security, which requires organizations to notify authorities of a breach within twenty-four hours of the event. This directive would require network defenders to review log information containing

it difficult for the end user to judge which standards are the best choice for their particular requirements.[37]

Proposed Solution(s). Few governments are considering incentives for rapid market adoption. Tax credits, subsidies, and rate recovery schemes provide faster paths to organizational participation and market adoption. For example, electric utilities are facing increased pressure to identify core cyber assets and increase the security and resiliency thereof.[38] This sector often has the ability to "pass" the cost on to its customers authorized by the government enabling them to "recover" cybersecurity investments. Of course, federal incentives like this only work for price-regulated industries when there is not further regulation at the state or municipal level.[39]

If governments want industry to invest in developing more secure products and services to prepare for the IoT, then a research tax credit should be

Well-meaning government officials do not always consider how a new policy, sometimes localized by country or region, could conflict with other existing policies.

personal, identifiable information. It is unclear which directive or standard takes precedence. More troubling is the fact that following one, if compelled by regulation, requires an organization or entity to break the law by not following the other. Finally, there are standards that are in conflict with one another and compete for adoption. This makes

considered. The research and experimentation credit in the United States Internal Revenue Code is one such example. Originally enacted in 1986, the research credit is one of many temporary provisions in United States tax laws that are routinely renewed by Congress. Because the research credit is focused on basic research, it could serve as an incentive for companies to apply their research agendas (and more importantly their money) toward developing products and services that are ket toward better security. The United States has already initiated the Federal Risk and Authorization Management Program (FedRAMP), a government-

Cybersecurity is an organization-wide risk area because it touches every Line of Business: the technology and fabric of the organization, its culture, brand and reputation, as well as legal and regulatory requirements.

well engineered, and therefore secure, resilient, and with few or no vulnerabilities.[40]

Of course, the government could also choose to apply subsidies to change the market conditions. For example, many governments provide an agriculture subsidy to farmers: to supplement their income, the government influences the cost of products like milk and corn, while managing the supply of such commodities. A cybersecurity subsidy could be used to incentivize ISPs to provide particular types of security and managed security services to businesses and citizens, thereby providing upstream security for downstream devices (as discussed earlier). The reduction in price to consumers or perceived "free service" would enhance security for all. This type of economic intervention may be required.

There is at least one other form of market incentive that proves effective: the power of demand. Security requirements should be part of the procurement and acquisition process.[41] For example, the government can use its purchasing power to influence the mar-

wide program that provides a standardized approach to security assessment, authorization, and continuous monitoring for cloud products and services. It is driving market behavior by demanding security through its procurement process.

Executive Accountability for Cyber is Required. It does not matter if you are a large retailer who has lost control of 100 million credit card numbers, or a large oil and gas company that has had 70 percent of its IT assets damaged, or an elementary school, or a farm. Cybersecurity constitutes a risk area for all organizations whether they acknowledge it or not. The challenge for each organization is at least two fold.

First, cybersecurity risk is a relatively new field. As a result, there is a lack of formal training, mutually agreed upon principles and measures, and actuarial tables to aid in appreciating its impact using empirical data. This is exacerbated when an organization delegates the responsibility for its cybersecurity *down* to the Chief Information Officer (CIO), whose main responsibility is to ensure the twenty-four/seven IT operations of the organization. Cybersecurity is an organization-wide risk area because it touches every Line of Business (LoB): the technology and fabric of the organization, its culture, brand and reputation, as well as legal and regulatory requirements. The only single place where accountability for all of the domains listed here is at the CEO level. Therefore, the only way to increase focus at scale across all industries is to shift to CEO level attestation and accountability.

Second, companies are coming under pressure from shareholders and governments to shore up their cyber defenses. In October 2011, the Securities and Exchange Commission (SEC) issued a notice to industry regarding cybersecurity. Public companies have existing obligations to disclose material risks and events on their public filings. A risk or event is considered a material one if it is important for the average investor to know before making an investment decision. Material risks can include cyber risks and material events can include cyber breaches, including the theft of intellectual property/trade secrets, penetrations that compromise operational integrity, etc. Because of past lack of reporting in this area, the SEC has issued guidance to clarify that in fact cyber risk and events should be reported to the Commission. In March 2014, the SEC convened a public meeting with all of its commissioners and Chairwoman Mary Jo White to underscore the importance of cybersecurity to the integrity of the market system and customer data protection. Ms. White further stated that the SEC intends to

move the guidance into a set of rules, and thus regulate industry to comply with the guidance.[42] The challenge for any company (private, public, employee owned, international) then, is that no framework has emerged yet to provide them with a "standard of due care" that they can attest to having met.

Proposed Solution(s). *Awareness and Accountability via Regulatory Influence*

Three independent agencies in the United States—SEC, the Federal Communications Commission (FCC), and the Federal Trade Commission (FTC)— have the ability to increase awareness about what is happening to our core infrastructure and drive, through regulation, an innovation agenda that can strengthen our information security posture.[43] For the purposes of this paper, we will focus on two. The SEC and the FCC have the authority to require publicly traded companies and telecommunications companies to attest to requirements for cybersecurity. If one or both were to require positive attestation for cybersecurity risk controls, then nearly 22,000 companies would do so.[44] If extrapolated across the world, then a significantly larger number of companies would be required to attest to controls.

Organizations' response to this requirement could be answers to questions posed at the C-suite level, from the Board of Directors to the CEO. A proposed, and manageable, list of questions would be:

- •Does the company understand the cybersecurity landscape and its relevance to the business sector(s)?
- •Does the company understand its networked environment (what

is connected, what it does, and to whom it is related)?

•Is cybersecurity part of the overall planning process with clearly delineated executive ownership of the process?

•Can the company demonstrate an adequate system of controls commensurate with the risk associated with its relevant business sector(s)?

•Does the company have a Computer Incident Response Teams (CIRTs) or capability with a formalized process to respond?

•Does the company have a disclosure process and has it followed it over (the last) period?

•Has the company established relationships with law enforcement or government officials to interdict or investigate incidents?

•Is there anything else we need to know?

In order to adequately answer these questions, a framework and practice—if not already in existence—need to be created. Today, information security frameworks such as the National Institute of Standards and Technology (NIST) CyberSecurity Framework v1.0, the British Standards Institute (PAS-555-2013), the Cyber Security Risk-Governance and Management Specifications, and the International Standards Organization (ISO) 27001/2, are too complicated and detailed to be reasonably applied and adopted at scale. ISO27001/2, for example, has over 110 controls, while the NIST CyberSecurity Framework v1.0 has 23 categories, and over 90 subcategories.

Today, most organizations do not apply, audit, and then certify to one of the existing frameworks.[45] If required (or regulated to use one of the existing frameworks) today, most organizations would find themselves unable to comply, and this would continue for quite some time. The impediments could include cost to certify, time to certify, inefficiency due to the complexity of existing frameworks, and inability to scale.[46] To overcome these challenges, we need to approach the problem differently. We need a framework and practice that manages risk in fewer domains with fewer questions, such as the Cyber Readiness Index — Enterprise Edition.[47] This framework is smaller, ensuring lower cost, quicker adoption, and flexibility to scale. Additionally, it is extensible, allowing for the addition of further requirements - improving over time and adapting to meet new needs. Finally, it allows organizations to mature their processes and operational implementation thereof, by setting the bar higher each time as opposed to setting a the highest standard that may not be initially achievable.

Conclusion. In our current state of cybersecurity, breach, crime, disruption, and destruction are growing in unacceptable ways. Key indicators suggest that we are not making enough progress and in fact, are possibly going backwards.

This paper proposed four actions to start taking *right* now. The four actions, revisited, are:

•Connected devices need minimum standards and enforcement;

•Security practice must return to the basics;

•The market needs additional influence; and

•Executive accountability for cyber is required.

It is time to adapt and adjust to the changing environment and anticipate the security requirements of the future Internet-connected world. An Internet Underwriters Laboratory (IUL), which tests and has the manufacturer test their products against cybersecurity requirements, would influence market behavior. Additionally, ISPs can and should provide upstream security for our downstream devices.

Security professionals need to return to the fundamentals, reducing the attack surface by taking proper care of the basic elements of cybersecurity: patching, upgrading, and testing. They also need to be diligent about eliminating dark space: detecting the "unknown devices" and "unknown connections" that provide safe haven for illicit and illegal activity. Additionally, decision makers need to start focusing on critical services, not critical infrastructures, because it will likely change their views and investments regarding protection, resilience, recovery, and restoration of assets.

Because cyber insecurity is growing, we need our governments to consider a broader range of market levers, including adopting incentives for rapid market adoption. Tax credits, subsidies, and rate recovery schemes all serve as options to affect market adoption and action.

Finally, organizations' executives and directors must be accountable and attest to requirements for cybersecurity.

We can no longer merely talk about these problems—we need to roll-up our sleeves and solve them. Meeting tomorrow's demands—increased network capacity, new applications, and an expanding base of users—requires anticipating next-generation security demands today. When the four areas of breach, crime, disruption, and destruction are contained and well-managed, we will have succeeded, but we have a great deal of work to do to get there.

Disclaimer: This paper was prepared and authored in the authors' personal capacity. The opinions expressed in this article are the authors' own and may or may not reflect the view of Cisco Systems, Inc, or any other affiliated organizations

NOTES

1 A data breach is an intentional or unintentional release of sensitive or secure information to an untrusted environment.

2 Verizon, 2014 Data Breach Investigations Report, 2014, p. 5, accessed June 21, 2014, http://www.verizonenterprise.com/DBIR/2014/ Ponemon Institute, 2013 Cost of Data Breach Study: Global Analysis, May 2013, accessed June 21, 2014, http://www.ponemon.org/local/upload/file/2013%20Report%20GLOBAL%20CODB%20FINAL%205-2.pdf.

3 Jose Pagliery, "Half of American Adults Hacked this Year," *CNN.com*, May 28, 2014, accessed June 21, 2014, http://money.cnn.com/2014/05/28/technology/security/hack-data-breach/index.html.

4 Ponemon Institute, 2013 Cost of Cyber Crime Study: United States, October 2013, p. 10, 13, accessed June 21, 2014, http://media.scmagazine.com/documents/54/2013_us_ccc_report_final_6-1_13455.pdf.

5 Ponemon Institute, 2013 Cost of Cyber Crime Study: United States, ibid.

6 Center for Strategic and International Studies (CSIS). "Net Losses: Estimating the Global Cost of Cybercrime". June 2014. (Page 6) , accessed June 21, 2014, http://csis.org/files/attachments/140609_rp_economic_impact_cybercrime_report.pdf

7 Commission on the Theft of American Intellectual Property, The IP Commission Report, May 22, 2013, accessed June 21, 2014, http://www.ipcommission.org/report/IP_Commission_Report_052213.pdf.

8 Software intended to damage a computer, mobile device, computer system, or computer network, or to take partial control over its operation.

9 IDC and the National University of Singapore, "The Link Between Pirated Software and Cybersecurity Breaches: How Malware in Pirated Software is Costing the World Billions" March 2014, p 2, accessed June 21, 2014, http://www.microsoft.com/en-us/news/downloads/presskits/dcu/docs/idc_031814.pdf.

10 Melissa E. Hathaway, "Change the Conversation, Change the Venue and Change Our Future," Centre for International Governance Innovation, May 13, 2013, accessed June 21 2014, http://www.cigionline.org/publications/2013/5/change-conversation-change-venue-and-change-our-future.

11 "Aramco Says Cyberattack Was Aimed at Production," *The New York Times*, December 9, 2012, accessed June 21 2014, http://www.nytimes.com/2012/12/10/business/global/saudi-aramco-says-hackers-took-aim-at-its-production.html?_r=0.

12 Bob Sullivan, "Spam in the Fridge: Hackers target home appliances," *MSN*, January 21, 2014, accessed June 21 2014, http://money.msn.com/saving-money-tips/post--spam-in-the-fridge-hackers-target-home-appliances.

13 Symantec, Internet Security Threat Report, April 2014, p. 7, accessed June 21 2014, http://www.symantec.com/content/en/us/enterprise/other_resources/b-istr_main_report_v19_21291018.en-us.pdf.

14 IHS, "More Connected than Ever: 6 Billion New Internet-Enabled Devices to Produced This Year," February 13, 2014, accessed June 21 2014, http://press.ihs.com/press-release/design-supply-chain/more-connected-ever-6-billion-new-internet-enabled-devices-be-prod.

15 David Bryan and Daniel Crowley, "Video: Hacking Home Automation Systems," *SC Magazine*, July 31, 2013, accessed June 21, 2014, http://www.scmagazine.com/video-hacking-home-automation-systems/article/305416.

16 A Secure Development Lifecycle (SDL) is a repeatable and measureable process to reduce product vulnerability, increase resiliency, and assure software and hardware. Vendors such as Microsoft, Cisco, and Oracle each have their own public versions of SDLs.

17 John N. Stewart, "Perspective: Not all Vendors and Products are Created Equal," *Georgetown Journal of International Affairs*, March 23, 2013, accessed June 21, 2014, http://journal.georgetown.edu/2013/03/23/perspective-not-all-vendors-and-products-are-created-equal-by-john-n-stewart/.

18 Microsoft, Linking Cybersecurity Policy and Performance, February 2013, accessed June 21, 2014, http://www.microsoft.com/en-us/download/details.aspx?id=36523.

19 Gartner, "Gartner Says the Internet of Things Installed Base Will Grow to 26 Billion Units By 2020," December 12, 2013, accessed June 21, 2014, http://www.gartner.com/newsroom/id/2636073.

20 Author's note: this came from a discussion with Alan Paller of SANS, some years back.

21 Daniel B. Klein, *Reputation: Studies in the Voluntary Elicitation of Good Conduct*, Economics, Cognition, and Society Series, (University of Michigan Press, May 15, 1997), 78.

22 Daniel B. Klein, ibid.

23 Daniel B. Klein, ibid, 78-79.

24 Melissa E. Hathaway and John E. Savage, "Stewardship of Cyberspace: Duties for Internet Service Providers," March 2012, p. 15, accessed June 21, 2014, http://belfercenter.ksg.harvard.edu/files/cyberdialogue2012_hathaway-savage.pdf

25 David McMahon, "Beyond Perimeter Defense: Defense-in-Depth Leveraging Upstream Security," in *Best Practices in Computer Network Defense: Incident Detection and Response* (IOS Press, February 2014).

26 Center for Problem Oriented Policing. http://www.popcenter.org/problems/child_pornography/4; and see: http://www.neowin.net/news/uk-isp-bt-broadband-to-block-porn-for-new-customers-by-default

27 The Information Warfare Monitor Project, "The Dark Space Project," 2012, accessed June 21, 2014, http://www.infowar-monitor.net/ and see http://www.dhs.gov/national-cybersecurity-protection-system-ncps and http://www.dhs.gov/sites/default/files/publications/privacy/privacy-pia-nppd-ncps.pdf.

28 Melissa E. Hathaway and John E. Savage, "Stewardship of Cyberspace: Duties for Internet Service

Providers," Ibid

29 Melissa E. Hathaway, "Advanced Research Workshop Findings," in *Best Practices in Computer Network Defense: Incident Detection and Response* (IOS Press, February 2014).

30 Danielle Walker, "GCHQ used fake LinkedIn, Slashdot pages to spy on Belgacom Employees," *SC Magazine*, November 11, 2013, accessed June 21, 2014, http://www.scmagazine.com/gchq-used-fake-linkedin-slashdot-pages-to-spy-on-belgacom-employees/article/320471/.

31 "Hotel scammers with fake wi-fi want your credit card information, *ABC News*, April 1, 2013, http://www.abcactionnews.com/news/local-news/i-team-investigates/hotel-scammers-with-fake-wi-fi-want-your-credit-card-information

32 John N. Stewart, "Advanced Technologies/Tactics, Techniques, Procedures: Closing the Attack Window, and Thresholds for Reporting and Containment," in Best Practices in Computer Network Defense: Incident Detection and Response (IOS Press, February 2014), http://www.cisco.com/web/about/security/intelligence/JNS_TTPs.pdf.

33 Secunia, Secunia Country Reports: Germany, 2014, http://secunia.com/resources/countryreports/de/.

34 SANS, SANS Critical Security Controls, 2014, http://www.sans.org/critical-security-controls/.

35 EU Directive on Network and Information Security; See: North American Electric Reliability Corporation (NERC) signed Order 791 on Critical Infrastructure Protection (version 5) Cybersecurity Standards; See: National Defense Authorization Act (NDAA) of 2013; See: Directive 95/46/EC Data Protection Directive.

36 Melissa E. Hathaway, "Toward a Closer Digital Alliance," *SAIS Review of International Affairs, vol. XXX*, no. 2 (November 18, 2010).

37 Melissa E. Hathaway, "Advanced Research Workshop Findings," Ibid.

38 Cyber Asset definition includes cyber assets that "if rendered unavailable, degraded, or misused would, within 15 minutes of its required operation, mis-operation, or non-operation, adversely impact one or more facilities, systems, or equipment." For more information on this, see: https://www.ferc.gov/whats-new/comm-meet/2014/032014/E-5.pdf.

39 Department of Homeland Security, "Executive Order 13636: Improving Critical Infrastructure Cybersecurity," June 12, 2013, http://www.dhs.gov/sites/default/files/publications/dhs-eo13636-summary-report-cybersecurity-incentives-study_0.pdf.

40 Melissa E. Hathaway, "Falling Prey to Cybercrime: Implications for Business and the Economy," in *Securing Cyberspace: A New Domain for National Security* (Aspen Institute Press, 2012) 145-157.

41 Securities and Exchange Commission (SEC), "Video: Cybersecurity Roundtable," March 26, 2014, http://www.sec.gov/news/otherwebcasts/2014/cybersecurity-roundtable-032614.shtml.

42 Securities and Exchange Commission (SEC), "Video: Cybersecurity Roundtable," March 26, 2014, http://www.sec.gov/news/otherwebcasts/2014/cybersecurity-roundtable-032614.shtml.

43 Melissa E. Hathaway, "Creating the Demand Curve for Cybersecurity," *Georgetown Journal of International Affairs, Special Issue* 2011: 163-170.

44 Credit Risk Monitor, "Directory of Public Companies in United States," (NASDAQ listing, NYSE listing, and

Company Index), http://www.crmz.com/Directory/CountryUS.htm.

45 Calculated by the number of corporations total minus the number attesting today.

46 Dejan Kosutic, "How much does ISO 27001 implementation cost?," *The Dejan Kosutic Blog*, February 8, 2011, http://blog.iso27001standard.com/2011/02/08/how-much-does-iso-27001-implementation-cost/.

47 Melissa E. Hathaway and John N. Stewart, "The Cyber Readiness Index- Enterprise Version 1.0," 2014.

The Private Sector

A Reluctant Partner in Cybersecurity

Amitai Etzioni

It may seem obvious that the private sector should be keen to protect its computers and networks from cyber-attacks by criminals and foreign agents. After all, hacking has caused considerable losses of trade secrets and other proprietary information. Moreover, evidence suggests that cyber-attacks can take a kinetic form, which can harm the equipment and facilities—such as the national electrical grid—of those attacked. However, as will be seen shortly, the private sector is far from rushing to protect itself from such attacks. The reasons for this reluctance range from the understandably pragmatic to the ideological. Meanwhile, in spite of major implications of this reluctance for homeland security, both the Bush and the Obama administrations have limited themselves to cajoling the private sector to embrace much stronger cybersecurity measures rather than mandating their introduction.

Threat Levels. Private sector firms suffer considerable damage from cybersecurity breaches. A report from the Center for Strategic and International Studies finds that the costs to the global economy—which encompass losses of intellectual property, outright cybercrime, unauthor-

Amitai Etzioni is a Professor of International Affairs and the Director of the Institute of Communitarian Policy Studies at George Washington University. Previously, he was a guest scholar at the Brookings Institution, a Senior Advisor to the White House, and has taught at Columbia University and Harvard Business School. In addition to attaining numerous academic awards, he has authored twenty-four books.

ized access to confidential business and stock information, the costs of recovering from cyber-attacks, and the value of reputational damages—of malicious cyber activity are "probably ... [as much as] $400 billion"—or even $1 trillion per year. The United States alone is estimated to suffer up to $120 billion in economic losses.[1] In 2012, one metallurgical corporation reportedly "lost technology to China's hackers that cost $1 billion and 20 years to develop."[2] In some cases, companies have been driven entirely out of business by Chinese hackers' persistent cyber espionage.[3] One report estimates that 508,000 American jobs have been lost due to cybercrime.[4] General Keith Alexander, until recently the director of the NSA and commander of United States Cyber Command, has estimated that economic espionage, including the kind practiced by Chinese and Russian hackers, represents "the greatest transfer of wealth in history."[5]

No industry is immune: cybersecurity firm Mandiant estimated in 2006 that cyber-attacks tied to China's People's Liberation Army (PLA) alone targeted twenty separate, major industries including telecommunications, energy, and aerospace.[6] Even Google—arguably one of the most sophisticated companies in the world with regard to computer networks—fell victim to a complex hack that originated in China, during which the hackers "appropriated some of Google's search engine source codes, a vital piece of intellectual property."[7]

These estimates of losses do not include the legal costs of data breaches and those resulting from consumer confidence; moreover, companies are often forced to pay fines when their cybersecurity measures fail to protect consumer information. Heartland Payment Systems, for example, was slapped with $150 million in fines and legal costs that stemmed from a 2007 cybersecurity breach in which more than 100 million credit and debit card numbers were illegally obtained by hackers.[8] One research institute estimated that malicious attacks cost American firms $277 per customer or user whose information was put in jeopardy by a company's cybersecurity failures.[9] Nevertheless, many corporations resist introducing many of the cybersecurity measures recommended by the U.S. government.

Reasons for Weak Private Sector Response.

The private sector's reluctance to adopt strong cybersecurity measures is driven by a combination of principles and practical concerns. Four of the most frequently articulated arguments against government mandated private sector cybersecurity standards follow.

First, significant segments of the private sector consider proposed requirements to introduce cybersecurity measures to be an additional form of government regulation. The Business Software Alliance opposes placing "undue regulatory burdens on industry," and the United States Chamber of Commerce opposes "legislation establishing regulatory-based cybersecurity standards."[10, 11] The Heritage Foundation opposed the same bill because it would "create a cumbersome regulatory process." These and other corporate leaders and economically conservative commentators adhere to the laissez-faire and libertarian principles that private enterprise has a right to be left alone by the government and that the private sector is capable of independently determining how much and what kind of cybersecurity it needs.

However, as James A. Lewis, a highly regarded cybersecurity expert at the

actions.[14] Therefore, it is unsurprising that CEOs and other executives seem to underestimate even the short-term consequences of failing to shore up cybersecurity. This problem is compounded by executives' inexperience

Ten years after the industry's conversation about private sector cybersecurity began, corporations continued to be inundated with cybersecurity breaches.

Center for Strategic and International Studies, points out, "The market *has failed* to secure cyberspace. A ten-year experiment in faith-based cybersecurity has proven this beyond question."[12] That is, ten years after the industry's conversation about private sector cybersecurity began, corporations continued to be inundated with cybersecurity breaches. Christopher Cox, former chairperson of the Security and Exchange Commission, put it more bluntly: "Voluntary regulation [of cybersecurity] does not work."[13]

Because corporations are considered rational actors, one might well expect that they would voluntarily take measures to protect their trade secrets and hence profits. The reasons they often do not are varied. For example, CEOs have been shown to focus on short-term costs and benefits, to the detriment of longer-term effects. The consequences of stolen trade secrets often take years to unfold because competitors need time to use the information they gained to build and market their own products. Moreover, humans tend to be poor at assessing the probabilistic costs of their

with technology. "Most [board members and executives] have gray hair," one banker and media executive said. "It's like having someone who has never paid any attention to their health talk to a doctor."[15] One expert on cybersecurity, meanwhile, writes, "Cybersecurity resembles environmental law in that both fields are primarily concerned with negative externalities. Just as firms tend to underinvest in pollution controls because some costs of their emissions are borne by those who are downwind, they also tend to underinvest in cyber-defenses because some costs of intrusions are externalized onto others."[16] Whatever the reasons, *The Wall Street Journal* writes that in the first six months of 2014 alone "1,517 U.S.-traded firms … have cited hacking as a business risk in filings," and that "federal officials and others say many companies remain ignorant of, and unprepared for, Internet intruders."[17]

Second, other opponents of government cybersecurity regulations claim that government mandates will actually hamper cybersecurity and other innovations in the private sector. In

2012, the United States Chamber of Commerce called on Senate Republicans to filibuster a bill that would have established cybersecurity standards for private sector critical infrastructure, on the grounds that the bill could actually "hamper companies trying to defend against cyber intrusions."[18] The argument seems to be that establishing clear standards for companies would impede their flexibility by forcing them to introduce cumbersome or inefficient cybersecurity measures.

Third, private sector representatives have suggested that cybersecurity regulations would impose substantial costs, which the private sector would be incapable of meeting profitably. A company would need to spend millions in order to develop effective cybersecurity systems.[19] Given that about 82,000 strains of malware were created daily in 2013, it would take large sums of money to "stay ahead of the curve."[20] Furthermore, "businesses consider it unfair and inappropriate for the government to impose on private industries security requirements that businesses consider a public-sector responsibility. Such requirements are viewed as 'unfunded mandates.'"[21] That is, corporate leaders argue that the provision of security is the job of the government; thus, they hold that if the government requires others to do part of the job by adding security measures above and beyond those they would already independently introduce, the corporations should be compensated for the related costs. However, these claims are hard to justify when one considers the sheer bulk of many private sector corporations' budgets: Target, the object of a notorious December 2013 breach, had a $1.6 mil-

lion cybersecurity system in place, true, but their revenues that year topped $72 billion—making their investment in cybersecurity roughly 0.0002% of their revenue.[22]

Fourth, the private sector has expressed concern that regulations mandating that corporations report cybersecurity breaches to the federal government and share news of cyber threats with their industry peers would cause them damaging publicity or lead to lawsuits alleging liability for damages to private citizens. One law office that provides corporate counsel wrote that Target's "potential total costs could reach over $1 billion" following a major cybersecurity breach in December 2013. Another source estimates that the cost of Target's failure could top $18 billion once lost revenues due to negative publicity are factored in.[23] When retailer Neiman Marcus suffered a similar security breach a few weeks later, it—and three other retailers—waited a month to notify customers, presumably in an effort to minimize negative publicity.[24]

In April 2014, the Senate introduced a bill that would incentivize private sector sharing of cybersecurity data by providing liability protection against lawsuits.[25] Senator Dianne Feinstein, chair of the Senate Intelligence Committee, stated that the bill "allows companies to monitor their computer networks for cyber-attacks, promotes sharing of cyber threat information and provides liability protection for companies who share that information."[26] However this bill has not been adopted.

Moreover, not all agree that the protection of corporations from liability will properly incentivize the private sector to adopt cybersecurity measures. Senator Jay Rockefeller has argued that offering "safe harbors" against liability for damages to third parties caused by breaches of cybersecurity in exchange

would have drawn on contributions from technology companies, and would have increased pressure on Internet companies to provide security technology with their products. However, these

Requirements were viewed as too onerous for business ... and ultimately anything that could offend industry, anything that hinted at government mandates, was stripped out [of legislation].

for company compliance with President Obama's new NIST Framework would not lead companies to develop dynamic, effective cybersecurity measures. Instead, "such an approach would likely have the opposite effect. ... Giving companies unprecedented liability protections based on cybersecurity standards that they themselves have developed would increase the likelihood that the American taxpayers will one day find themselves on the hook for corporate bailouts of unknown scope following a cyber disaster."[27]

A Reluctant Federal Government.

In face of strong private sector opposition, the federal government has largely resorted to cajoling the private sector to implement cybersecurity measures and has eschewed mandatory regulation. Stewart Baker, who served as Assistant Secretary for Policy at the Department of Homeland Security, has described the fate of cybersecurity proposals advocated by Richard Clarke, the first White House cybersecurity czar. According to Baker, the proposal "sidled up toward new mandates for industry, would have formed a security research fund that

requirements were viewed as too onerous for business by many within the Bush administration, and ultimately anything that could offend industry, anything that hinted at government mandates, was stripped out.[28] One bill proposed by Congress initially "called for mandatory minimum security standards" for the private sector, but the Chamber of Commerce and other corporate representatives opposed the regulations. To salvage the bill's chances of passing, it was rewritten to advocate voluntary standards; nonetheless, the bill failed.[29] And President Obama, in a 2009 address regarding cybersecurity policy, explicitly stated, "My administration will not dictate security standards for private companies."

Instead, the federal government has recently taken a number of preliminary steps to encourage the private sector to adopt more stringent cybersecurity measures. In August 2013, it identified a number of possible incentives that could be used to entice the private sector to adopt cybersecurity best practices, including "cybersecurity insurance, federal grants, and legal protections for companies that invest additional money in cybersecurity efforts."[30] The government also offered sixteen critical infrastructure sectors guidance about how to shield themselves from cyberattacks, but did not mandate compliance with its recommendations.[31] The General Services Administration, in conjunction with the Department of Defense, recommended that private sector entities be required to comply with "baseline" cybersecurity principles at all levels of the supply chain as a condition of being awarded contracts with the federal government.[32] However, this recommendation has not been adopted. Several pieces of legislation have been proposed in Congress to either sanction private sector entities that fail "to adopt 'reasonable' data security practices" or to grant the Federal Trade Commission authorization to craft cybersecurity regulations for the private sector.[33] However, like other

ernment should focus on protecting its computers and networks, especially those that belong to the Departments of Defense and Homeland Security, the Central Intelligence Agency, and the Federal Bureau of Investigation. This is, in effect, the position that the Bush and Obama administrations have followed. However, this approach ignores that considerable amounts of defense and homeland security work are carried out by the private sector.

For fiscal year 2013, the federal government awarded a total of $460 billion in contracts, much of which seems to have gone to defense contractors.[34] In 2010, the Department of Defense spent about $400 billion of its $700 billion annual budget on private contractors that provided vehicles, armor, weapons, transportation, logistical support, and many other goods and services, which ranged from aircraft

Inadequate cybersecurity at private firms allows adversarial governments and nongovernmental actors to acquire information that could greatly harm U.S. defense and homeland security.

proposed legislations in the five years, these drafted bills have not yet become law. Cybersecurity in the private sector, as this section has demonstrated, remains far from satisfactory.

Implications for Homeland Security. One might hold that if the private sector fails to protect itself from cyberattacks, it will suffer the consequences and eventually mend its ways. The same line of thinking suggests that the gov-

carriers and nuclear submarines to hand grenades and MREs. The federal government also outsources much of the work of intelligence collection and analysis to private sector contractors. About "one in four intelligence workers has been a private contractor, and 70 percent or more of the intelligence community's secret budget has gone to private firms," according to a *Washington Post* report.[35] And private security firms such as Blackwater—which has since been renamed Xe Services and, later, Academi—were contracted to protect diplomats, offer counterterrorism training, and supplement U.S. military forces in Iraq and elsewhere.[36, 37]

Thus, inadequate cybersecurity at private firms allows adversarial governments and nongovernmental actors to

includes information technology, used by the government. The computers and software used by the Department of Defense—and other federal agencies—are themselves designed, manufactured, and often serviced by the private sector. Prior to the 1990s, the Pentagon used in-house programmers to design

There can be no reliable cybersecurity in the public realm unless there is also heightened cybersecurity in the private realm.

acquire information that could greatly harm U.S. defense and homeland security. To cite a recent example, on May 19, 2014, Attorney General Eric Holder Jr. announced charges against five members of the People's Liberation Army's Shanghai cyberunit and alleged that the hackers infiltrated the computer networks of several American corporations.[38] Among these were Allegheny Technologies, which provides "materials and components" to a diverse group of clients including defense contractors; and Alcoa, which manufactures a range of materials used in defense.[39] In the past, General Dynamics, Boeing, Lockheed Martin, Raytheon, and Northrop Grumman—the United States' leading defense contractors—have all fallen victim to hackers.[40] And a cyber-espionage operation against Lockheed Martin in 2007 made it possible for China to steal design details of the F-35 Lightning II, which were subsequently used to develop China's J-20 stealth fighter plane.[41]

Second, the private sector is responsible for supplying and maintaining much of the technology, which

secure software tailored to the military's needs. However, the military has since increasingly shifted to off-the-shelf commercial software as a means of cutting costs and satisfying Congress, which seems to be influenced by private sector lobbying.[42] These technologies are vulnerable not only because they are produced in the private sector, but also because the private sector often sources its equipment and components overseas—which includes China.

Third, the private sector is responsible for the maintenance of much of the United States' critical infrastructure, including energy, telecommunications, transportation, health services, and banking and finances, among others. Without the private sector's willing adoption of stronger cybersecurity measures, these critical services remain vulnerable to kinetic cyber-attacks. On June 6, 2014, the Financial Stability Oversight Council released a report that shows that the financial industry is vulnerable to cyber-attacks. It held that "cyber incidents that disrupt, degrade, or impact the integrity and availability of critical financial infrastructure … [could] threaten the stability of the financial system."[43] Another June 2014 report from the Government Accountability Office cautioned that "maritime security plans required by law and regulation generally [do] not identify or address potential cyber-related threats." Thus, private "maritime stakeholders" at U.S. ports, which handle more than $1.3 trillion in goods per year, remain vulnerable to cyber-attacks, which could shut down business communications, disable physical security systems, and more.[44]

In short, the difference between the public and private sectors is much smaller than is often assumed in public discourse.[45] There can be no reliable cybersecurity in the public realm unless there is also heightened cybersecurity in the private realm. The security chain is only as strong as its weakest link—and the private sector's link is simultaneously poorly forged and critically important to U.S. defense and security.

What can be done? The private sector, especially those firms that manufacture defense items such as submarines and aircraft carriers as well as those that provide hardware and software to the government, would be much more attentive to cybersecurity needs if the federal government were to disqualify from receiving government contracts corporations that are not in full compliance with government cybersecurity standards. President Obama's 2013 Cybersecurity Executive Order has called for this step, and the White House has directed a joint working group to "develop an implementation plan for these recommendations."[46] However, this strong corrective assumes a different political climate, in which Congress, which is rather responsive to corporate lobbying, would allow the administration to set standards and develop blacklists. At the moment, such blacklists are not even drafted for corporations that are found to engage in corruption. One government agency might cease to grant a corporation contracts, but there is no list of corrupt corporations that other agencies can consult. The publication of articles like this one combined with increased public outcry on the subject might help change the political climate and advance cybersecurity.

NOTES

1 James Lewis and Stewart Baker, "The Economic Impact of Cybercrime and Cyber Espionage," Internet, http://www.mcafee.com/us/resources/reports/rp-economic-impact-cybercrime.pdf (date accessed: 29 June 2014).

2 Michael A. Riley and Ashlee Vance, "China Corporate Espionage Boom Knocks Wind Out of U.S. Companies," Internet, http://www.bloomberg.com/news/2012-03-15/china-corporate-espionage-boom-knocks-wind-out-of-u-s-companies.html (date accessed: 29 June 2014).

3 James A. Lewis, "China's Economic Espionage," Internet, http://www.foreignaffairs.com/articles/138427/james-a-lewis/chinas-economic-espionage (date accessed: 29 June 2014).

4 Sid Kircheimer, "Cybercrime Costs 508,000 U.S. Jobs," Internet, http://blog.aarp.org/2013/07/25/cybercrime-costs-508000-u-s-jobs/ (date accessed: 29 June 2014).

5 Joshua Phillip, "The Staggering Cost of Economic Espionage Against the US," Internet, http://www.theepochtimes.com/n3/326002-the-staggering-cost-of-economic-espionage-against-the-us/ (date accessed: 29 June 2014).

6 Carrie Lukas, "It's Time for the U.S. to Deal with Cyber-Espionage," Internet, http://www.usnews.com/opinion/articles/2013/06/04/chinas-industrial-cyberespionage-harms-the-us-economy (date accessed: 29 June 2014).

7 Jamil Anderlini, Peter Marsh, John Reed, Joseph Menn, Peggy Hollinger, and Daniel Schäfer, "Industrial espionage: Data out of the door," Internet, http://www.ft.com/intl/cms/s/0/ba6c82c0-2e44-11e0-8733-00144feabdc0.html#axzz35DQLxMz4 (date accessed: 29 June 2014).

8 Danny Yadron, "Companies Wrestle With the Cost of Cybersecurity," Internet, http://online.wsj.com/news/articles/SB10001424052702304834704579403421539734550 (date accessed: 29 June 2014).

9 The Economist, "White hats to the rescue," Internet, http://www.economist.com/news/business/21596984-law-abiding-hackers-are-helping-businesses-fight-bad-guys-white-hats-rescue (date accessed: 29 June 2014).

10 Business Software Alliance, "Security," Internet, http://www.bsa.org/advocacy/security (date accessed: 29 June 2014).

11 However, the U.S. Chamber of Commerce endorsed the Cybersecurity Act of 2013, which "would codify NIST's role in developing the Cybersecurity Framework." Hogan Lovells Privacy Team, "U.S. Cybersecurity Policy Developments: A Year-to-Date Roundup," Internet, https://www.privacyassociation.org/privacy_tracker/post/u.s._cybersecurity_policy_developments_a_year_to_date_roundup (date accessed: 29 June 2014).

12 James A. Lewis, "Innovation and Cybersecurity Regulation," Internet, http://csis.org/files/media/csis/pubs/090327_lewis_innovation_cybersecurity.pdf (date accessed: 29 June 2014). Here, faith-based refers to the assumption that the private sector will act in good faith to secure its networks and computers against cyber-attacks.

13 James A. Lewis, "Innovation and Cybersecurity Regulation," Internet, http://csis.org/files/media/csis/pubs/090327_lewis_innovation_cybersecurity.pdf (date accessed: 29 June 2014).

14 Daniel Kahneman, *Thinking, Fast and Slow*, New York: Farrar, Straus and Giroux, 2011.

15 Danny Yadron, "Boards Race to Fortify Cybersecurity," *The Wall Street Journal* (date accessed: June 30, 2014).

16 Nathan Alexander Sales, "Regulating Cyber-Security," *Northwestern University Law Review* 107, no. 4 (Summer 2013): 1508.

17 Danny Yadron, "Boards Race to Fortify Cybersecurity," *The Wall Street Journal* (date accessed: 30 June 2014).

18 Ken Dilanian, "U.S. Chamber of Commerce leads defeat of cyber-security bill," Internet, http://articles.latimes.com/2012/aug/03/nation/la-na-cyber-security-20120803 (date accessed: 29 June 2014).

19 Danny Yadron, "Companies Wrestle With the Cost of Cybersecurity," Internet, http://online.wsj.com/news/articles/SB10001424052702304834704579403421539734550 (date accessed: 29 June 2014).

20 Kevin Coleman, "Meeting the cost of cyber-security," Internet, http://www.defensenews.com/article/M5/20140325/C4ISRNET18/303250028/Meeting-cost-cybersecurity (date accessed: 29 June 2014).

21 Amitai Etzioni, "Cybersecurity in the Private Sector," *Issues in Science and Technology* 28, no. 1 (Fall 2011): 58-62.

22 Alexander Botting, "Cybersecurity in the private sector — playing catch-up," Internet, http://thehill.com/blogs/congress-blog/technology/205883-cybersecurity-in-the-private-sector-playing-catch-up (date accessed: 29 June 2014).

23 Emily R. Caron, "Target Data Breach and NIST Cybersecurity Framework Raise Tough Insurance Questions," Internet, https://law.ku.edu/sites/law.ku.edu/files/docs/media_law/2014/Media_Privacy_Beyond.pdf (date accessed: 29 June 2014).

24 Ariel Yehezkel and Thomas Michael, "Cybersecurity: Breaching the Boardroom," Internet, http://www.sheppardmullin.com/media/article/1280_MCC-Cybersecurity-Breaching%20The%20Boardroom.pdf (date accessed: 29 June 2014).

25 Alina Selyukh, Ros Krasny, and Chris Reese, "Senate Cybersecurity Bill Gives Firms Liability Protection for Sharing Data," Internet, http://www.insurancejournal.com/news/national/2014/04/30/327968.htm (date accessed: 29 June 2014).

NOTES

26 Alina Selyukh, Ros Krasny, and Chris Reese, "Senators ready to try again on U.S. cybersecurity legislation," Internet, http://www.reuters.com/article/2014/04/30/us-usa-cybersecurity-congress-idUSBREA3T0QF20140430 (date accessed: 29 June 2014).

27 Alex Wilhelm, "Sen. Rockefeller blasts granting firms liability protection for following voluntary cybersecurity standards," Internet, http://thenextweb.com/us/2013/06/05/sen-rockefeller-blasts-granting-firms-liability-protection-for-following-voluntary-cybersecurity-standards/ (date accessed: 29 June 2014).

28 Amitai Etzioni, "The Bankruptcy of Liberalism and Conservatism," *Political Science Quarterly* 128, no. 1 (Spring 2013): 39-65. Internal quotation marks omitted.

29 Ken Dilanian, "U.S. Chamber of Commerce leads defeat of cyber-security bill," Internet, http://articles.latimes.com/2012/aug/03/nation/la-na-cyber-security-20120803 (date accessed: 29 June 2014).

30 Grant Gross, "Feds explore cybersecurity incentives for private sector," Internet, http://www.computerworld.com/s/article/9241407/Feds_explore_cybersecurity_incentives_for_the_private_sector (date accessed: 29 June 2014).

31 Alexander Botting, "Cybersecurity in the private sector – playing catch-up," Internet, http://thehill.com/blogs/congress-blog/technology/205883-cybersecurity-in-the-private-sector-playing-catch-up (date accessed: 29 June 2014).

32 Trisha Leon, "U.S. Launches Initiative for Procurement Cybersecurity," Internet, http://www.bsminfo.com/doc/u-s-launches-initiative-for-procurement-cybersecurity-0001 (date accessed: 29 June 2014).

33 Alexander Botting, "Cybersecurity in the private sector – playing catch-up," Internet, http://thehill.com/blogs/congress-blog/technology/205883-cybersecurity-in-the-private-sector-playing-catch-up (date accessed: 29 June 2014).

34 Danielle Ivory, "Federal Contracts Plunge, Squeezing Private Companies," Internet, http://www.nytimes.com/2014/01/16/business/federal-contracts-plunge-squeezing-private-companies.html (date accessed: 29 June 2014).

35 Robert O'Harrow, Jr., Dana Priest, and Marjorie Censer, "NSA leaks put focus on intelligence apparatus's reliance on outside contractors," Internet, http://www.washingtonpost.com/business/nsa-leaks-put-focus-on-intelligence-apparatuss-reliance-on-outside-contractors/2013/06/10/e940c4ba-d20e-11e2-9f1a-1a7cdee20287_story.html (date accessed: 29 June 2014).

36 The Associated Press, "Case Against Contractors Resurfaces," Internet, http://www.nytimes.com/2013/10/18/us/case-against-contractors-resurfaces.html?_r=0 (date accessed: 29 June 2014).

37 Jeremy Scahill, "Blackwater's Secret Ops," Internet, http://www.thenation.com/article/154739/blackwaters-black-ops# (date accessed: 29 June 2014).

38 Michael S. Schmidt and David E. Sanger, "5 in China Army Face U.S. Charges of Cyberattacks," Internet, http://www.nytimes.com/2014/05/20/us/us-to-charge-chinese-workers-with-cyberspying.html (date accessed: 29 June 2014).

39 Bill Gertz, "Indictment of China Military Hackers Reveals New Details of Cyber Attack Methods," Internet, http://freebeacon.com/national-security/obama-administration-indictment-of-army-hackers-seeks-to-deter-cyber-attacks/ (date accessed: 29 June 2014).

40 Eloise Lee and Robert Johnson, "The 25 Biggest Defense Companies In America," Internet, http://www.businessinsider.com/top-25-us-defense-companies-2012-2?op=1 (date accessed: 29 June 2014).

41 Bill Gertz, "Top Gun takeover: Stolen F-35 secrets showing up in China's stealth fighter," Internet, http://www.washingtontimes.com/news/2014/mar/13/f-35-secrets-now-showing-chinas-stealth-fighter/?page=all (date accessed: 29 June 2014).

42 Richard A. Clarke, *Cyber War: The Next Threat to National Security and What to Do About It* (New York: Harper Collins, 2010).

43 Financial Stability Oversight Council, "2014 Annual Report," Internet, http://www.treasury.gov/initiatives/fsoc/Documents/FSOC%202014%20Annual%20Report.pdf (date accessed: 29 June 2014).

44 United States Government Accountability Office, "Maritime Critical Infrastructure Protection: DHS Needs to Better Address Port Security," Internet, http://www.gao.gov/assets/670/663828.pdf (date accessed: 29 June 2014).

45 Amitai Etzioni, "The Bankruptcy of Liberalism and Conservatism," *Political Science Quarterly* 128, no. 1 (Spring 2013): 39-65.

46 "Cybersecurity: Coming Soon to a Government Contract Near You," Internet, http://www.venable.com/cybersecurity-coming-soon-to-a-government-contract-near-you-02-04-2014/ (date accessed: 30 June 2014).

Cybersecurity Investments in the Private Sector

The Role of Governments

Lawrence A. Gordon, Martin P. Loeb, and William Lucyshyn

The Internet has given rise to a burgeoning digital world-wide economy that goes way beyond what most could have imagined a few decades ago. Customers can buy products from firms around the world, and competitors can enter worldwide economic markets without many of the barriers to entry that plague traditional economic markets based on a brick-and-mortar presence. Many refer to this new economic model as a flat world of commerce (e.g., see Friedman, 2006). Unfortunately, as with most phenomena in life, there are both positive and negative features of this new world order of commerce. The introduction of new cybersecurity risks concomitant to conducting business in the cyber domain is one of the most notable of the negative aspects. While evolving technologies (e.g., cloud computing) may appear to reduce cybersecurity risks, other evolving technologies employed by attackers (be they lone wolf hackers, organized criminals, terror organizations, or nation states) ensure that technology cannot eliminate the cybersecurity risks faced by businesses.

Recent high-profile cybersecurity breaches at major multinational retail stores (e.g., Target, Inc.) prompted a February 4, 2014 U. S. Senate Judiciary Committee hearing

Lawrence A. Gordon is a Professor of Managerial Accounting and Information Assurance at the Robert H. Smith School of Business and an Affiliate Professor at the Maryland Cybersecurity Center at the University of Maryland.

Martin P. Loeb is a Professor of Accounting and Information Assurance at the Robert H. Smith School of Business and an Affiliate Professor at the Maryland Cybersecurity Center at the University of Maryland.

William Lucyshyn is a Research Director at the Defense Advanced Research Projects Agency (DARPA), and is a Visiting Senior Research Scholar at the Center for Public Policy and Private Enterprise and Affiliate Researcher at the Maryland Cybersecurity Center at the University of Maryland.

and gained wide media coverage.[1] The coverage highlighted the cybersecurity risks confronting businesses, as well as the risks to consumers. Regretfully, 100% security is neither feasible nor economically justified even if it were viable. The above notwithstanding, corporate executives need to determine the amount their firms should invest in cybersecurity. Indeed, deciding the appropriate level to invest in cybersecurity related activities has become a critical concern for senior corporate executives. Furthermore, oversight of firms' cybersecurity activities is now on the agenda of corporate Boards of Directors (Yadron, 2014).

This article has two objectives. First, this article will point out the unique problems associated with deriving the appropriate level of cybersecurity investments by profit-oriented corporations. As will become clear, corporate underinvesting in cybersecurity activities is both systemic and not easily resolved. Second, this article will discuss policies that governments could and should adopt in order to foster increased investments in cybersecurity related activities by profit-oriented corporations.

Cybersecurity Investments in Profit-Oriented Corporations.

Profit-oriented corporations make all kinds of investments related to their business on a regular basis. Investments in buildings, technology-based equipment, computer software, personnel, and marketing are just some of the areas where executives regularly make investment decisions. Global corporations also typically make decisions regarding activities such as mergers and acquisitions. Investment decisions are generally made on a cost-benefit basis, under the rubric of what corporate executives usually refer to as "making the business case."[2] A key aspect of the "business case" process is quantifying the benefits associated with the potential investment opportunities. Since most corporate investment opportunities focus on generating new revenues for the firm, the benefits from most investment opportunities are specified in terms of anticipated incremental revenues. These anticipated incremental revenues are translated into cash flows for discounted cash flow (DCF) analyses.[3] Investment opportunities of this nature are usually referred to as revenue generating investments. Given that financial markets (especially the stock market) focus on revenue growth for firms, senior executives are always searching for new revenue generating investment opportunities.

Revenue generating investment opportunities are not, however, the only type of investment opportunities available to senior executives. Cost savings (or cost avoidance) investments are another category of corporate investment opportunities. Cost savings investment opportunities focus on accomplishing a particular task in a more cost efficient manner than was previously available to the corporation. A classic example of a cost savings corporate investment opportunity is replacing legacy manufacturing equipment with more modern, high-tech, equipment that significantly reduces the labor intensity of the manu-facturing process. In such a case, the firm may be able to justify, and verify on an *ex post* basis, the return on the investment based on the cost savings in terms of cash flows (for DCF analyses) resulting from a sub-stantially lower payroll expense.

savings exacerbates both the *ex ante* and *ex post* evaluation of cybersecurity investments, making the investment evaluation process for cybersecurity investments qualitatively different than the evaluation of other types of risky investments. Consequently, the markets for transferring risks are not as well established for cybersecu-

The markets for transferring risks are not as well established for cybersecurity investments... [this] makes the business case for cybersecurity investment decisions a much tougher sell to senior manage-ment...

Cybersecurity investment oppor-tunities are generally a unique class of cost savings investments.[4] For the most part, investments in cybersecu-rity activities are directed at avoiding the costs associated with cyberse-curity breaches. What makes this class of investments unique is that the cost savings cannot be directly verified on an *ex post* basis. If a cybersecurity investment is success-ful, the cost savings comes from avoiding the non-observable cyber-security breach. Thus, the *ex post* cost savings for cybersecurity investment opportunities need to be comput-ed based on the difference between some sort of *ex ante* prediction of what the costs of security breaches would have been without the incre-mental cybersecurity investment and what the costs of security breaches actually turned out to be.[5] The lack of actuarial data on the actual cost

rity investments as they are for most other investments. Not surprising-ly, this situation makes the busi-ness case for cybersecurity invest-ment decisions a much tougher sell to senior management than typical cost savings projects, let alone rev just enue-generating projects.[6] As a result, there is a strong tendency for firms to underinvest in cybersecurity activities unless some sort of major security breach occurs (see Gordon et al., 2003a).

Another aspect of underinvest-ment in cybersecurity activities in profit-oriented corporations has to do with *externalities*. Externalities refer to the spill-over effects of an activity. In other words, externalities are the costs (or benefits) to firms or indi-viduals that arise from actions taken by another firm or individual that are not borne by the firm or individ-ual taking the action. In the context of corporations underinvesting in cybersecurity activities, externalities usually refer to the costs associated with weak cybersecurity protection borne by firms other than the initial firm that is underinvesting in cybersecurity activities. More specifically, firms that underinvest in cybersecurity activities only absorb the private costs resulting from a cybersecurity breach. These private costs would include the costs to detect and correct a cybersecurity breach, as well as any decreased revenues due to lost customers. In addition, any costs associated with legal liability incurred by a firm experiencing a cybersecurity breach could be a private cost to the firm. In contrast, the costs borne by supply-chain partners of the firm experiencing a cybersecurity breach, however, are not entirely absorbed by the firm that underinvests in cybersecurity activities. For exam-

their supply-chain partners, means that these externalities often extend far beyond national borders.

The combination of cybersecurity investments being unique cost-savings projects, and the externalities associated with cybersecurity breaches, have created a situation whereby corporate underinvesting in cybersecurity activities is both systemic and not easily resolved through free economic markets.

Government's Role in Corporate Cybersecurity Investments.

The systemic tendency for corporations to underinvest in cybersecurity activities is, in part, the direct result of the extraordinary difficulties of justifying cybersecurity investments based on cost-benefit analysis (i.e., making the business case) relative to other corporate investment opportunities. Furthermore, the fact that corporations are

There is currently a market failure, wherein a free economic market is unable to generate an efficient allocation of resources.

ple, underinvesting in cybersecurity by the initial firm can result in the inadvertent transfer of malware or vulnerabilities to a partnering firm, thereby causing a reduction in the partnering firm's current and future sales and profits. This reduction in the partnering firm's sales and profits is the result of externalities (i.e., spill-over effects of the poor cybersecurity by the initial firm). The global reach of most firms, and

only attuned to the private costs, while ignoring costs associated with externalities, also leads to corporate underinvestment in cybersecurity activities. This underinvestment increases the risk that a cyber attack may take down an entire critical infrastructure industry (i.e., electric generation), causing critical damage to both a nation's economy and its national defense.

The situation described above demonstrates that there is currently a market failure, wherein a free economic market is unable to generate an efficient allocation of resources. Market failures often result in a situation where government intervention is desirable. In other words, governments are often able to play an important role where free economic markets fail. This role could be based on encouraging the adoption of voluntary actions by profit-oriented corporations (as is the generally preferred role within the U.S.)[7] or requiring mandated actions (as seems to be the emerging approach in Western Europe).[8] There are several actions available to governments around the world to support a more efficient allocation of corporate resources to cybersecurity activities. The most obvious of these actions are discussed below.

Support for Education on Conducting Cost-Benefit Aspects of Cybersecurity Investments

As discussed, the primary benefits derived from investments in cybersecurity activities are the result of the cost-savings that result from avoiding or minimizing cybersecurity breaches. These savings, however, are not directly observable. Consequently, managers arguing for additional cybersecurity funds need to be able to develop estimates of the cost of cybersecurity breaches to their firm on an *ex ante* basis. The use of econometric models, as well as non-quantitative analyses (e.g., analytic hierarchy process), can be extremely valuable in making these estimates.

Managers arguing for cybersecurity investment funds need to understand how to combine the various risk factors (i.e., threats, vulnerabilities, and potential losses) into a meaningful

framework for allocating cybersecurity resources. For example, a threat/vulnerability value grid could be developed to facilitate the handling of the risk associated with potential cybersecurity breaches (Gordon and Loeb, 2011).[9]

The difficulties associated with estimating the cost savings from cybersecurity investments and considering the various risk factors presents an exceptionally challenging situation for those responsible for securing cybersecurity investment funds. This situation is further complicated by the fact that many managers responsible for implementing their firms' cybersecurity activities and proposing new cybersecurity projects have a background in technology, but little financial management training. Thus, these managers face a relative disadvantage in competing with financially savvy managers for project funding within the firm. Accordingly, governments can play an important role in rectifying this situation by supporting financial management training. Governments can reduce the underinvestment in cybersecurity activities by facilitating the education of cost-benefit analysis for cybersecurity investments. Governments should, in cooperation with universities and/or private sector firms, establish cybersecurity cost-benefit training programs for corporate executives.

Support for Corporate R&D on Cybersecurity

Research and development (R&D) on ways to combat cybersecurity threats are essential to cybersecurity. Corporations' willingness to invest in R&D, however, faces a number of obstacles. First, the payoffs from such investments are highly uncertain and are therefore often discounted heavily. Second, to the extent R&D efforts are successful, there are positive externalities that accrue to firms not making the initial investment (i.e., a large part of successful R&D often becomes a public good).[10]

Governments can play an important role in the R&D cybersecurity arena, with a particular emphasis on government-corporate and government-academic partnerships. Such partnerships could and should cross national borders in that governments from various countries can join forces to support various research projects. A key concern is transferring the technological advances derived from the R&D into practical use by corporations. Govern-

sidies increase the overall corporate investments in cybersecurity activities, there are obvious benefits to the firms receiving the subsidy, as well as to their corporate partners (i.e., there are positive externalities).

Incentives for Information Sharing

Information is critical to the prevention, detection, and response to cyber-attacks. The relevant information, though, is dispersed among many organizations, including network operators, information systems hardware and software providers, law enforcement, and government intelligence organizations. Consequently, information sharing is critical to effective cybersecurity. "For example, dur-

One of the most important steps to improving cybersecurity, particularly on a global scale, is for governments to develop and implement incentives that encourage more effective sharing of information related to cyber threats, vulnerabilities, and best cybersecurity practices.

ments can accelerate this process with the judicious use of funds and sponsorship, as has been done by the Department of Homeland Security.[11]

Subsidies for Corporate Cybersecurity Investments

Governments could provide a direct subsidy (e.g., tax credit) for corporate cybersecurity investments along the lines of subsidies offered for other corporate activities (e.g., investments in energy efficient manufacturing processes). To the extent that such sub-

ing the denial-of-service attacks that targeted the websites of many leading U.S. banks over the last few years, the Financial Services Information Sharing and Analysis Center brought these banks together to exchange information with each other and with the Federal government" (Daniel, 2014). In the absence of appropriate incentive mechanisms, however, private sector firms often attempt to free ride on the cybersecurity expenditures of other firms, hoping to benefit from information of other firms, but refusing to share their private information (Gordon et al. 2003b). One of the most important steps to improving cybersecurity, particularly on a global scale, is for governments to develop and implement incentives that encourage more effective sharing of information related to cyber threats, vulnerabilities, and best

often just pointing out the fact that a serious cybersecurity breach could have a negative impact on the firm's business.

The above noted Disclosure Guidance has moved corporations registered with the U.S. SEC toward improved transparency concerning cybersecurity risks and incidences. The movement

The global nature of economic markets, combined with the fact that a firm's information and system security is only as strong as its weakest link, means that cybersecurity needs to be treated as a global, rather than national or local, issue.

cybersecurity practices.[12]

Support for Transparency of Corporate Cybersecurity Risks

In 2011, the U.S. Securities and Exchange Commission (SEC) came out with its Disclosure Guidelines concerning the importance of firms reporting their cybersecurity risks and cyber incidents on their Annual 10-K Reports (SEC, 2011). Prior to this Disclosure Guidance, a small percentage of the SEC registrants were already providing information on their cybersecurity related activities (see Gordon et al, 2006, 2010). However, since the issuance of the 2011 Disclosure Guidance, nearly all firms are reporting some aspect of cybersecurity risks and/or cyber incidences in their 10K reports (often under Section 1A, titled Risk Factors). The above notwithstanding, much of the information provided tends to be of a boiler-plate nature,

thus far, however has been modest at best. Accordingly, we agree with the opinion expressed by Senator Rockefeller in his April 9, 2013 letter to the SEC Chairperson, where he noted that the 2011 Disclosure Guidance was an important first step, but "... given the growing significance of cybersecurity on investors' and stockholders' decisions, the SEC should elevate this guidance and issue it at the Commission level as well. While the staff guidance has had a positive impact on the information available to investors on these matters, the disclosures are generally still insufficient for investors to discern the true costs and benefits of companies' cybersecurity practices" (Rockefeller, 2013). The SEC should also suggest that corporations specify the dollar amount of their expenditures on cybersecurity activities (i.e., similar to what is done with capital expenditures). Furthermore, the global nature of corporations (including the fact that their stakeholders come from all over the world) requires an international movement toward corporate reporting of cybersecurity related activities and risks.

Global Cybersecurity Standards

The global nature of economic markets, combined with the fact that a firm's information and system security is only as strong as its weakest link, means that cybersecurity needs to be treated as a global, rather than national or local, issue. Although efforts do exist to establish global standards for cybersecurity (e.g., see ISO 27001, a standard for an Information Security Management System), these efforts have not been very effective to date. Given that cybersecurity issues are a relatively new issue confronting corporations, the lack of generally accepted and adopted global cybersecurity standards is unsurprising. Nevertheless, the establishment of global cybersecurity standards seems to be a necessary, though not sufficient, condition for eventually winning the cybersecurity battle.

One factor overlooked by most proponents of global cybersecurity standards is that a framework for developing and implementing such standards may already exist. A related situation exists in connection with developing and implementing global accounting standards. Ever since the early 1970's, businesses and governments have discussed the benefits of and need for international accounting. It was not until around the establishment of the International Accounting Standards Board (IASB) in 2001, however, that the movement finally gained momentum. Over 120 countries have adopted the International Financial Reporting Standards (IFRS) that the IASB issues.[13] The parallels between the benefits of IFRS and the benefits from a potential international cybersecurity standards (ICS), suggest an IASB type framework for the development and establishment of ICS. A good starting place might be the implementation of an International Cybersecurity Standards Board along the lines of the IASB.

Governments, as a major consumer of goods and services, could begin by limiting their purchases to those firms complying with such global standards. As an interim step, governments could enforce such a purchasing rule based on national cybersecurity standards. It should be noted, however, that while cybersecurity standards may go a long way to improve cyber hygiene and offer protection against less sophisticated attacks, they are not without their drawbacks. In particular, standards can take years to develop, coordinate, and implement, but threats and supporting technologies change on a timescale of days, weeks, and months. Moreover, there are situations whereby imposing a standard may result in a firm redirecting cybersecurity funding away from a more productive security activity to a less productive security activity in order to meet the standard, thereby reducing the firm's overall level of cybersecurity.

Concluding Comments. Cybersecurity has become a major concern to profit-oriented corporations. Given the rapid development of the digital and social networking revolution, there can be little doubt that managing cybersecurity risks will play an ever increasing role in managing the overall risks of firms. There are systemic reasons related to how profit-oriented corporations make investment decisions that explain why corporations tend to underinvest in cybersecurity activities. Corporate unwillingness to invest adequately in cybersecurity activities represent a market failure, resulting in significant cyber risks that spill over to other corporate and non-corporate entities. In addition, corporate underinvestment in cybersecurity activities put worldwide economies and the military defense of nations at risk. Governments could and should assume more active roles to facilitate greater corporate focus on cybersecurity related activities.

NOTES

1 For the C-Span.org coverage of the Senate hearing, where Mr. John Mulligan, the Chief Financial Officer and Senior Vice President of Target, Inc., answered questions concerning the cybersecurity breach, see: http://www.c-span.org/video/?317553-1/hearing-cybercrime-privacy.

2 Making the business case refers to the process of identifying various opportunities, developing data to support the various opportunities, selecting the most profitable (i.e., highest return) opportunity and allocating resources to that opportunity (see Gordon and Loeb, 2006, Chapter 6).

3 DCF analyses are technique excused by economists for the purpose of computing either a net present value or internal rate of return on an investment opportunity (see Gordon and Loeb, 2006, Chapter 2).

4 Although it is possible for a cybersecurity investment to generate new revenues for a firm, due to some sort of competitive advantage, this aspect of cybersecurity investments is usually of insignificant consequences relative to the cost savings aspects of cybersecurity investment decisions.

5 Moreover, cybersecurity breaches are not always detected, thus, making the measurement of the savings from the cybersecurity investment even more troublesome.

6 Since financial markets (especially stock markets) tend to focus on revenue growth as a key indicator of corporate growth, revenue-generating projects are clearly preferred over cost-savings projects by most senior executives.

7 The U.S. government has developed a new Framework (NIST 2014) for improving cybersecurity of the nation's critical infrastructure, which adopts a voluntary risk-based approach. The Framework is intended to be a living document, that will evolve over time and it identifies five cybersecurity functions: identify, protect, detect, respond, and recover. The objective is to assist firms in critical infrastructure sectors to identify key cybersecurity risks and issues, and help them assess their ability to respond to cyber-attacks. Ideally, the firms can then evaluate the need for improvements.

8 The European Union is moving toward a more broad and direct approach, for example, by directing common minimum requirements for the Network and Information Security at the national level (Euorpean Commission 2013).

9 The Gordon and Loeb (2011) article, in *The Wall Street Journal*, provides a non-mathematical approach to using the Gordon-Loeb Model (see: http://en.wikipedia.org/wiki/Gordon-Loeb_Model) for cybersecurity investments. See Gordon and Loeb (2002) for the original technical presentation.

10 A public good is a good in which its availability for consumption is unaffected by its consumption by any individual and no individual can be excluded from its consumption.

11 The U.S. Department of Homeland Security (DHS) has taken a lead in supporting R&D partnerships with academicians and corporations, as well as in facilitating multinational support for such projects (see http://www.dhs.gov/csd-new-projects).

12 In a recent policy document, the Justice Department regulators explained that sharing of cyber-threat information differs from the sharing of competitive information, such as pricing data and business plans, and is not a violation of anti-trust laws (Wyatt 2014).

13 It is interesting to note that the U.S. is one of the countries that has not yet adopted IFRS, although the U.S. SEC does allow foreign registrants to use IFRS for the purpose of SEC reporting. For an excellent summary of the history of the SAB and IFRS, go to the FASB website at: http://www.fasb.org/jsp/FASB/Page/SectionPage&cid=1176156304264.

Country in Focus

National Cyber Security Strategy

Are We Making Progress? Japan's Efforts and Challenges

Yoko Nitta

No nations' security strategies are currently prepared for cyber attacks. These attacks are advancing dramatically and are increasingly more threatening than cyber espionage, which governments have been typically involved with. Cyber attacks impact individuals and industries, as well as thwart national defense and social order. Cyber warfare refers to offensive exchanges of military, political and diplomatic intelligence, which can target national defense systems and critical social infrastructure. Now, the use of cyber capabilities is a growing trend in warfare, especially to augment other military components. Cyber policy is now an integral aspect of foreign policy issues ranging from human rights to national security.

There is a global increase of cyber-attacks traversing state borders, which makes international cyber security cooperation vital for global security. Cyber-cooperation, however, is not new for Japan, as the Asian state recently signed an agreement with the United States. Moreover, the Japanese cyber industry is constantly advancing and is a strong national resource, which raises domestic demands for international cyber defense cooperation. The demand for international cyber security agreements demonstrates that cyber defense

Yoko Nitta is a senior principal researcher at the Japan Society for Security and Crisis Management, where she focuses on science diplomacy, cyber espionage, information warfare and intelligence. She was a former associate fellow at the Japan Science and Technology Agency (JST), as well as a professional investigator with Japan's Ministry of Foreign Affairs.

is one of the biggest security challenges of the 21st Century. It is apparent that states believe international cooperation is key to increase their ability to solve the challenge.

In this regard, observations of Japan's cyber security strategy and its approach to international collaboration for cyber issues will be laid out.

Risks to Global Commons. The National Security Strategy of Japan, which got approved at the ministry level in December 2013, describes cyber-space as a global common: cyberspace, a global domain comprised of information systems, telecommunications networks and others, provides a foundation for social, economic, military and other activities. Meanwhile, the risks of cyber-attacks that intend to steal classified information, disrupt critical infrastructure and obstruct military systems are becoming more serious. In Japan, the increasing level of interconnected networks of social systems and various other elements makes cyber space valuable for promoting both economic

efforts in comprehensively proofing cross-cutting measures to defend cyber-space and strengthen its response capabilities against cyber-attacks to protect its networks from malicious activities, ensure the free and safe use of cyber-space, and guard its critical infrastructure, including those in which Japan suspects adversarial state involvement. To this end, Japan will strengthen public-private partnerships to assess the risks of network systems' designs, developments and operations. It will further identify incidents, minimize their damages and their expansion, and analyze their causes to prevent similar incidents in the future. In addition, Japan will comprehensively consider and take necessary measures with regard to expanding the pool of human resources in the security field, protecting control systems, and responding to issues of supply chain risk. Furthermore, Japan will strengthen inter-agency cooperation and define the roles of relevant agencies so that it can reinforce its capabilities to protect cyberspace and respond to nation-wide incidents. At

The strategy touches upon strengthening and expanding Japan's capabilities and the roles of Japanese cybersecurity contributions overseas.

growth and innovation through the free flow of information. Protecting cyber-space from the above-mentioned risks is vital to maintain national security.

The strategy also touches upon strengthening and expanding Japan's capabilities and the roles of Japanese cybersecurity contributions overseas: Japan as a whole will make connected

the same time, Japan will promote a range of measures, including enhancing its ability and function to oversee, assess, apprehend, analyze, and internationally coordinate responses to cyber incidents, as well as reinforcing relevant agencies in charge of those tasks. In promoting these measures, strengthening international partnership in a wide range of areas is essential. For this, Japan will take measures at technical and operational levels to enhance collaboration with other countries. Japan will also strengthen information sharing and promote cyber defense cooperation with relevant allies.

There is another challenge; it has become increasingly important for nations to speak with a unique voice and advance a global vision of cyber space, which has produced conflicts among some states. Russia and China have different perspectives from those of the United States and other countries regarding the free flow of information. It is next to impossible that Japan could fill the gap for the time being.

Background. There was motivation for Japan to wake-up from its peaceful past seventy years to the current uncertain and insecure situation. To begin with, Mitsubishi Heavy Industries, one of the biggest Japanese defense corporations, got cyber attacked and information was stolen from their eleven offices in Japan. To make matters worse, Mitsubishi Heavy Industries did not report their attacks to the Ministry of Defense (MOD), even though they are a prominent defense contractor.

This was followed by an unconfirmed information leakage at the Japan Nuclear Energy Safety Organization (JNES), an attack case on TPP-related information at the Ministry of Agriculture, Forestry and Fisheries of Japan (MAFF), external unauthorized access to servers at the Japan Aerospace Exploration Agency (JAXA), a zero-day attack causing particular entities to be infected by web browsing at government agencies, and the possibility of an information leakage by a virus infection at the Japan Atomic Energy Agency (JAEA). Later, the National Information Security Center (NISC) aimed to coordinate and take charge of particular ministries and agencies. NISC was launched under the Cabinet Office in April 2005 as a control tower of Japanese information security policies.

Additionally, Big Data has high economic potential and has been discussed at the ministry level for its use as a driver for economic growth. Corporations have already incorporated it as their competitive tool. Big Data is a common platform for information sharing and its data is regarded as a service because open data, initially stored knowledge, M2M (streaming data) and personal data can be collected and replaced with Big Data. On the other hand, the characteristics of cyber space may cause Big Data to increase the severity of risks, dissemination of risks, and the globalization of those risks. Unfortunately, the method of compiling data is impossible to predict in advance so that it is difficult to know the potential risk in advance. Japan may be overlooking the challenges that Big Data poses—including the way companies interpret the information, manage the politics of data and find the necessary talent to make sense of the flood of new information.

Big Data, in other words, introduces high stakes into the data-analytics game. There is a greater potential for privacy invasion, greater financial risk exposure in fast-moving markets, greater potential for mistaking noise for true insight, and a greater risk of spending lots of money and time chasing poorly defined problems or opportunities. Unless

Japan understands and deals with these challenges, it risks turning all that data from something that has the potential to benefit Japanese organizations into a diversion, an illusion or a paralyzing turf battle.

The Defense Posture Review Interim Report published by the Ministry of Defense (MOD) has shown the new integrated mechanism of the Self Defense Forces (SDF), combining the forces of Air, Marine and Land to combat cyber attacks. This new task force, the Cyber Defense Unit, was launched at the end of March 2014. The report serves as a basis for the new National Defense Program Guidelines that motivates Japan's medium and long-term defense policies.

The Japanese government will also redesign the National Defense Program Guidelines, which will be published at the end of 2014, which will be a trigger for a big leap. The new guideline should be pragmatic and promote mutual interests between the United States and Japan.

Analysis for Japan Cybersecurity Strategy.

The Japanese Cybersecurity Strategy covers diverse areas. The three main pillars are: (1) a resilient cyberspace to strengthen ability of protection and recovery among all stakeholders, (2) a vigorous cyberspace to strengthen creativity and knowledge through developing technology, capacity building, and increasing public literacy, and (3) a world-leading cyberspace to strengthen the ability of contribution and outreach through diplomacy, global outreach and international cooperation.

The National Information Security Council (NISC) is responsible for managing the ministries working on cyber attacks. This conglomeration is going to be redesigned as a Cyber Security Center with strengthened authority by the end of 2015. The Center has laid out a mid-term goal by Fiscal Year 2015 to increase cyber security information-sharing among government agencies and critical infrastructure providers, decrease malware infection rates and citizen concerns, and improve international incident coordination, as well as a long-term goal by 2020 to double the size of the domestic information security market and increase the proportion in security professionals in the marketplace.

1)*Is the strategy focused towards a particular type of threat?*

The strategy is focused on attacks against our critical infrastructure, such as critical industry information, which is our source of global competitiveness and benefits corporations, academia, and research and development institutions that deal with intellectual property and piracy information. A significant threat is also cyber attacks toward state secrets. There is a need to strengthen the ability to recognize and to respond to cyber attacks against these critical assets.

2)*Has Japan outlined the necessary steps, programs and initiatives that must be undertaken to address the threat?*

The Control System Security Center (CSSC) is at ethnology research association to conduct R&D to handle cyber attacks and ensure the security of control systems of critical infrastructures that support people's lives, such as gas and power plants. In order to ensure the security of control systems of impotent infrastructures, CSSC conducts various thorough operations including research and development, international standardization, certification, human resource development, and the security verification of each system. On 17 May 2013, eighteen corporations joined the association to contribute to control systems security research, edification, education, training, authentication and international collaboration. It is a critical issue for the national security and risk management complex to deal with cyber attacks against control systems of important infrastructures, such as gas and power plants.

Another Japanese technology project to deal with cyber attacks is a cyber attack alert system, which the National Institute of Information and Telecommunication Technology (NICT) developed. Termed the "NICT Daedalus Cyber- attack alert system", this project views the state of an attack on networks visible in "3D" real-time graphics. Daedalus, which stands for "Direct Alert Environments for Darknet and Livenet Unified Security," visualizes large groups of computers from multiple perspectives to track any suspicious activity as it moves through the network. Today's cyber attacks breach boundary defenses of organizations internally and externally, which includes spreading malware via USB memory sticks (this could be most lethal weapon in the twenty- first century), mail attachments, as well as zero-day exploits. Therefore, using Daedalus along with conventional boundary systems is expected to improve organizations' network security. NICT also provides the system free of charge to educational institutions.

The challenge is that if Japanese critical infrastructure gets attacked, it is difficult for the Ministry of Defense (MOD) and Self Defense Forces (SDF) to adequately respond, since the new cyber response unit only consists of 90 people as of today. While its structure will be strengthened, the response unit's main mission is to protect the network system of MOD and SDF. Furthermore, it is a quite challenging to determine who attacks via attribution, and whether we can respond. Plus if the attacker is a single person, it is uncertain whether the military should respond. The upcoming Japan-U.S. Guidelines will address these issues.

3)*Has a responsible entity or competent authority been identified in Japan's Cybersecurity Strategy? Is that entity or authority empowered?*

Critical infrastructure industries interact with the Cyber Security Information Sharing Partnership of Japan (J-CSIP, pronounced JAY-sip), which takes initiative for cyber security information-sharing partnership between Ministry of Education, Science and Technology, Culture and Sports (MEXT) and private sector. The Information-Technology Promotion Agency (IPA) operates this cyber-security partnership. IPA collects information on cyber attacks that are detected at member companies and their group companies, anonymizes the information source (the member company who provided the information), obscures or deletes sensitive information, adds its own analysis, makes the information sharable with the authorization from the information source, and shares the information with member companies. Additionally, Japan's Computer Security Incident Response Team (CSRIT) works on detection, triage and response. Its mission is quite similar to that of firefighters. CSIRT is a critical operations model and its daily training and accumulated knowledge is an asset.

Japan has also sent SDF to the United States to train their cyber defense skills and bring their cyber security knowledge back home. Japan and the United States held the first working level meeting over cyber defense to prepare for launching the project in 2015. The two nations confided in each other that cyberspace cooperation would require constructing a working-level panel over the issue. The panel intended to discuss cyber attack training and considered dispatching commander-class officers from cyber-related units to one another's instructors in each country.

The NISC has the Government Security Operation Coordination Team (GSOC) to monitor computer systems protect the secrecy of telecommunications. Due to these articles, telecommunications cannot be traced down nor analyzed without contractual agreements between users and carriers, even if illegal correspondences are found in the telecommunication network. As a result, it is difficult and time-consuming to block or cease those illegal telecommunications. A recent example is a computer that was remotely attacked with a virus last year. NPA's response to the incident was inadequate, and eventually NPA arrested the wrong person for the attack. This indicates that there are no laws in place to effectively collect communication records, even though countries overseas possess those laws and regulations. It is also quite difficult to identify the criminal with a surveillance camera. In order to bolster Japan's attribution and track-

> **There are no laws** in place to effectively collect communication records, even though countries overseas possess those laws and regulations.

of ministries, collect information on incidents, and analyze them on a 24/7 basis. Each ministry in the Japanese government has a Computer Security Incident Response Team.

4) *Are the laws adequate?*

The National Policy Agency (NPA) has been doing everything they can to deal with cyber attacks under the current law. However, the current legal framework to promote robust Japanese cybersecurity is inadequate. Article 21 of Japanese Constitution and article 4 of Telecommunication Business Act ing of cyber-threats, it is necessary to develop a legal framework that grants certain governmental institutions the authorities to inspect and analyze network data. It is therefore essential that articles of the Japanese constitution and Japan's telecommunications business law be changed. Because Japan is an island nation and connected through submarine cables via landing points, the country should be able to tap into these network lines to watch malicious communications.

5) *Has funding been set aside to address the*

cyber security shortfalls? What are the highest priorities and why?

The Japanese government does not collect enough information on cyber attacks since there is no sufficient information-sharing mechanism based on trust similar to what the United Kingdom has. Japanese corporations are rather reluctant to report to government due to fears of publicizing their gaps in cybersecurity. Exposing institutional weakness could result in profit-losses from falling stock prices and investor uncertainty. Accordingly, Japan needs to define beforehand which information should be confidential and solely for government, as well who can access their corporate network data.

Another concern is that most of the software used to combat cyber attacks in Japan is manufactured overseas. If a new, domestically made system can be created for monitoring communication activity, it would be a huge leap for Japanese cybersecurity.

More importantly, Japan needs to foster human resources and put them on well-established positioning to advance Japan's cyber security strategy. Providing adequate funding and incentives for all these requirements is essential to attain this goal.

The Challenge of Cyberspace: Living and Working in a Digital Society.

Humankind has taken for granted the pervasiveness of computerization and the equally ubiquitous connectivity of what we have come to call cyberspace. In just over twenty years, society has become massively dependent on the benefits of what has grown into a vast and complex global information and communication system. The system that allows us to effortlessly withdraw cash anywhere in the world, video chat with loved ones on the other side of the globe, or connect to the office while traveling in the wilderness is one aspect of cyberspace, while Edward Snowden's leaking of the National Security Agency's details of United States global surveillance operations, and the widespread use of cyberspace by criminal organizations and ordinary individual criminals is another. Yet there are divergent views on whether to prioritize or ignore the dark side of the contemporary communications revolution. Humanity not only produces vast amounts of information, but it also routinely allows that information to be accessed by others, sometimes for good and sometimes for malign purposes.

On the positive side, "data analytics" (often describe as "Big Data") is facilitating major strides in improving productivity and efficiency in areas as diverse as "smart" electricity grids, genomic medicine and personal digital assistants. Massive Open Online Courses (MOOCs) offer a fundamental shift in the democratization of education and its outreach to those in emerging economies.

On the negative side, there is the widespread criminal use of cyberspace and a burring of the boundaries between state and non-state actors in activist attacks and old-style espionage, but with constantly evolving tools. Similar abuses of the privacy of personal data, especially in sensitive areas such as medical records, could fundamentally undermine trust between a government and its citizens.

Further Implications. Governments use cyberspace for a variety of purposes, both defensive, to counter the exploding number of cyber attacks on government agencies, and offensive, such as the Stuxnet worm attacks on the Natanz facility in Iran in 2010. The increasing tendency to see cyberspace as a battlespace and computers as weapons can be best seen in the October 2012 statement by the then-Secretary of Defense, Leon Panetta, who declared that cyber warfare- conflict between states or non-state actors using attacks on, with, and by computers- is the greatest threat facing the United States.

Even though we have not yet developed many of the capabilities that are being bruited, there are nonetheless those who worry about a "cyber Pearl Harbor" that will attack infrastructure targets built in the pre-computer age. Trying to provide security against the possibility of a cyber attack seems to be a constant challenge by government agencies charged with providing their

deepen the control of governing elite. Similarly, these deeply interconnected and interdependent elements have a tendency to form "accidental systems" whose characteristics are poorly understood and may weaken both technological and social resilience through potential cascades of failure.

Conclusion. While the technologies underpinning cyberspace have been through some forty years of continuous exponential growth in performance per unit price, humans remain linear beings; they do not adapt well on the same timescale. This points to a key area where more work is required. The growing impact on individual citizens and organizations by these developments is poorly understood. Good security is a holistic balance of personnel security, physical security and electronic security. In many organizations, excessive testing in the (nonetheless important) technological approaches to cybersecurity has led to neglect of the other

Abusing the privacy of personal data, especially in sensitive areas such as medical records, could fundamentally undermine trust between a government and its citizens.

citizens with protection. The creation of a Cyber Command by the United States in 2010 is one such measure.

Yet it is not just the "weaponization" of cyberspace that has engaged governments and security agencies. In many countries, governments use the Internet and their citizens' apparent addiction to cyber-connectivity to

areas with potentially disastrous results. Some organizations, by focusing too much on the technological approaches to cyber security, were neglecting some of the basics of physical security and personal security. Failing to hire new staff and failing to check the authenticity of biographies in job applications is one such example. There is also a poor understanding across general pollutions of the basics of "cyber hygiene." Even the fundamental tools of business lag behind. As a consequence, we fail to apply many tried and tested corporate disciplines to these new challenges. The increased use of social media continues to transform politics in countries around the world, posing challenges to long-established political institutions.

In the one year since the cybersecurity strategy was passed, Japan has been successfully developing its cyber capabilities as well as struggling to implement certain crucial provisions. With adequate support, resources, and clearly established policy and legal frameworks, Japan will achieve new heights in cyber security for years to come.

NOTES

1 National Information Security Council "Japan Cybersecurity Strategy"

June 13, 2013 http://www.nisc.go.jp/active/kihon/pdf/cybersecuritystrategy-en.pdf

2 National Information Security Council "International Strategy on Cybersecurity Co-operation ~ J-initiative for cybersecurity" October 2013 http://www.nisc.go.jp/active/kihon/pdf/InternationalStrategyonCybersecurityCooperation_e.pdf

3 The Government of Japan "National Security Strategy of Japan " December 2013 http://www.cas.go.jp/jp/siryou/131217anzenhoshou/nss-e.pdf

4 Defense of Japan 2013 'White Paper' http://www.mod.go.jp/e/publ/w_paper/2013.html

5 Richard A. Clarke and Robert K. Knake's "Cyber War: The Next Threat to National Security and What to Do About It" (Harper Collins, 2010)

Military Matters

The Command Imperative
Crafting Protocols for Cyber Conflict

Jarno Limnéll

The here-and-now threat posed by cyber weapons and their virtually inevitable role in every significant conflict around the globe is acknowledged throughout the U.S. defense establishment. What we decidedly lack, however, are proven command and control strategies for cyber conflict; protocols and rules of engagement; and sufficient game theory for predicting outcomes. The immature world of cyber warfare lacks Kissingers and Brzezinskis. Filling these voids should be an urgent defense priority for the United States and its allies.

Our situation with cyber weapons today is in some respects comparable to that of the stewards of nuclear weapons in the 1950s. The technology is known to work, though its full — especially indirect — consequences and knock-on effects are not yet fully grasped.

But when it comes to managing cyber capabilities, the twentieth century nuclear experience provides limited instruction. Many more actors have cyber capabilities, and some are literal outlaws who cannot be held liable to be present for civilized arms control talks. Unlike nuclear assets, cyber weapons are deployed against opponents virtually constantly at a whole spectrum of intensity levels.

Jarno Limnéll is Director Cyber Security at McAfee, part of Intel Security, Intel Corporation, where he researches cyber security and international politics. Prior to joining McAfee, Dr. Limnéll served a long career as an officer in the Finnish Defense Forces.

In the nuclear age it took decades to generate control protocols. With cyber weapons, firm schools of thought are still gelling. We should regard every political or military standoff as a learning lab for cyber strategists—in Spring 2014 the Russia-Ukraine conflict offered useful lessons—as well as all the world's major events, from Olympic games to national elections.

The Fifth Domain. Cyberspace is widely acknowledged as the fifth domain of warfare—joining land, sea, air, and outer space. A century ago, World War I militarized the air, and soon no nation regarded its security as complete without an air force; today, cyberspace inspires a similar race to mobilize. NATO established its Cyber Defense Centre of Excellence in Tallinn, Estonia in 2008[1] after "Web War I," a prolonged cyber onslaught against Estonian banks, media, and government assets that coincided with an argument with Russia over the fate of Tallinn's Bronze Soldier Soviet war memorial.[2] U.S. Naval Academy midshipmen today

gress in early 2014 that the United States remains unprepared for hostilities in this fifth sphere. "We have a lot of infrastructure—electric, our government, our financial networks," said Alexander. "We have to have a defensible architecture for our country, and we've got to get on with that."[4]

Why is it proving so challenging to devise command and control protocols for cyber weapons? There are several practical, tactical answers, and at least one philosophical one.

Practical Obstacles. The tools for waging a conventional kinetic conflict are typically in the hands of nation-states. The tools for fomenting cyber-chaos belong to a much broader, more ragged set of players. Hacktivist culture occurs underground in societies, even when hackers may perform as contracted proxies for a provocateur state. Some of the most creative and resourceful, as well as the most toxic and eradicative minds in cyber warfare operate in the shadows. The key players simply will not be rounded up or ever cajoled to nego-

Some of the most creative and resourceful, as well as the most toxic and eradicative minds in cyber warfare operate in the shadows.

break from seamanship studies to pass courses on digital network architecture with live hacking exercises. The Pentagon has had a formal Cyber Command (CYBERCOM) since 2010 with a classified mandate to defend U.S. cyber assets.[3]

Yet the first head of CYBERCOM, General Keith Alexander, told Con-

tiate protective conventions.

Another problem at least the U.S. government faces is scarce cyber talent. Credible command-and-control systems require a certain level of institutional stability to promote shared belief. Talent "churn" in the ranks is detrimental, as is the gnawing sense that the best and brightest individuals migrate elsewhere in search of greater material rewards.

U.S. Defense Secretary Chuck Hagel seeks to expand the Pentagon's Cyber Mission Force from its current 1,800 headcount to 6,000 by 2016. "To continue recruiting and retaining talent...we must build rewarding, long-term cyber career paths. Our military must enable our [people] to reinvent themselves for life in and beyond their service," said Hagel in March 2014.[5] But it is hard for DoD to compete with Silicon Valley's eye-popping job offers.

What Has War Turned Into? Now
for the philosophical point: the ethical construct that undergirds traditional kinetic conflict—which holds that war is justified only as a defensive response to aggression—is upended somewhat in the fifth domain.

War has traditionally been an armed contest for territory. Cyber war, however, borrows the stealthy nature and methodology of spying, which is a quest for knowledge, and is typically entrepreneurial as well as defensive. Military or terroristic aggression as we know it endangers and ends lives. But cyber aggression jeopardizes bank accounts, water and electricity supplies, air traffic control, traffic and transit systems, and certainly military networks. Disrupting any of these may convulse a civilian population efficiently, but would it justify like-for-like cyber retaliation from the victim state, or escalation to a kinetic response? And against whom? To whom does the international community address liability for nationalist cyber-activism when an apparent, logical culprit state plausibly denies responsibility?

Conflict in the fifth domain of cyberspace enlarges the definition of "war" to encompass espionage, sabotage, opinion influencing, and intellectual property theft. It gives nations new ways to pursue their political goals on the world's chessboard. We are entering a dangerously unstable and suspicious era without a roadmap of tested command-and-control fundamentals.

Ethics theorists Patrick Lin, Fritz Allhoff, and Neil Rowe have argued that the good cyber warrior's hands may be tied. "[I]t becomes difficult to justify military response to a cyber attack that does not cause kinetic or physical harm as in a conventional or Clausewitzian sense, such as the disruption of a computer system or infrastructure that directly kills no one. Further, in cyberspace, it may be difficult to distinguish an attack from espionage or vandalism, neither of which historically is enough to trigger a military response. For instance, a clever cyberattack can be subtle and hard to distinguish from routine breakdowns and malfunctions."[6]

Because cyber warfare is convoluted and interwoven into the fabric of modern hostilities involving state or non-state "freelance" actors, the ethicists' time-honored "just war theory" may be edging toward obsolescence. Future international conflicts may be ever more vaguely defined, with no clear beginnings or ends, no declarations of victory or surrender. They may just burn on and on beneath the surface of the visible world. (Human participants may not even be aware; software may do all the fighting.)

"Somehow, cyber warfare slips through the net of just war theory and it proves to be quite difficult to regulate using old, traditional ethical principles," says Mariarosaria Taddeo, a University of Warwick research fellow specializing in cyber security. "Just war theory is an ethical theory concerned with the preservation and respect for human life and liberty; it is all about

enemy. These little thrusts tend to be ongoing; they equate to everyday espionage. During diplomatic disputes or worse, however, the number and variety of attacks increase.

Small attacks can make a big difference. When publicly noted, they can degrade public trust in crucial systems,

We are entering a dangerously unstable and suspicious era without a roadmap of tested command-and-control fundamentals.

limiting casualties and physical damage... In the grand scheme of just war theory there is no place for informational infrastructures, data and information. In other words, there is no concern for the targets of cyber warfare."[7]

The more ominous cyber capabilities grow, the more troubling are our command-and-control knowledge gaps. There is much still to understand about the escalation patterns and ripple consequences of cyber war. Cyber planners' highest strategic priority today should be data acquisition. Every significant conflict or political event on the planet is a figurative classroom, as it is likely to include an element of cyber conflict.

Three Tiers of Cyber Conflict. It is possible to hypothesize three discrete, increasingly disruptive levels of cyber hostilities, each requiring a different command and control approach.

The first category of cyber conflict is the "business as usual" level — DDoS (denial of service) attacks and similar crude, blunt-force incursions. Website disruptions exert minor pressure on an

put leaders on the defensive, and have the potential, as we shall see, to fracture the open global Internet.

This tier of cyber conflict frustrates military command-and-control architects in multiple ways. The multilateral, thrust-and-parry nature of these attacks is anything but programmatic. A purely defensive "goaltender" posture can overtax home resources and ultimately fail some of the time anyway. Additionally, first-category attacks often show evidence of outsourcing to subcontractors. Cyber attacks on Ukraine during the March 2014 Crimea referendum appeared to originate with mercenaries or Russian-backed "patriotic hackers," rather than the armed forces or spy apparatus.[8]

As noted earlier, hiring hacktivists affords a government plausible deniability of involvement in cyber assaults. (It may also convey an impression of popular support for the state's position, as the attacks can be portrayed as private, spontaneous efforts.)

Borrowing from kinetic warfare's command-and-control playbook to wage this level of cyber conflict is probably fruitless, like trying to dispatch a swarm of hornets with a handgun. However, monitoring and analyzing small attacks, growing the knowledge base, and sharing findings with stakeholders are all important. At this level, information-sharing is the key to a successful defense.

The second category of cyber conflict is concentrated information operations, or INFOOPs, across Internet channels. INFOOPs refer to propaganda and disinformation campaigns to shift or inflame public opinion. They take more strategic planning, creativity, and intellect than primitive first-category attacks, but can do more damage, at least of a social and political nature. The cyber side of INFOOPS is a case of new bottles, old wine — but how apropos the new bottles of the Internet prove for this sort of exercise. With its numberless tribalist cells-cum-echo chambers, the web is a natural substrate for propaganda. Disinformation specialists infiltrate online communities and social media, making it harder for the online population to discern the truth.

The Russians, originators of agitprop, must find the Internet a natural and irresistible arena, and indeed fought and won a multi-channel "information war" during the run-up to the Crimea vote. "Skewed facts, half-truths, misinformation and rumors all work in the propagandist's favor," said the UK Guardian, noting the barrage from Moscow of televised and printed disinformation.[9] There were reels of scripted interviews and doctored images.

"An excellent propaganda apparatus, such as the Russian one, can find ways to repeat its message over and over again in slightly different ways and formats," says Yale University historian Timothy Snyder, who has written extensively on the Russia-Ukraine conflict. "If people in free societies have their discussions framed for them by rulers of unfree societies, then they will not notice the history unfolding around them (a revolution just happened in Europe!) or sense the urgency of formulating policy in a desperate situation (a European country has just invaded another!). Propaganda can serve this technical purpose no matter how absurd it is."[10]

Many of us have had the experience of otherwise level-headed, perspicacious friends relaying Internet "facts," from spurious photos of pony-sized cats to outlier conspiracy rants, that somehow attain more gravity for them by dint of having come to them online or via social networks rather than on TV or in a newspaper. Cyber warriors are now using this mysterious credibility aura to further political goals.

The most ominous reading of this level of cyber hostility is as an overt prelude to conventional military attack. This was Snyder's view of the Crimea cyber campaign: "Propaganda is thus not a flawed description, but a script for action. If we consider Putin's propaganda in these Soviet terms, we see that the invasion of Crimea was not a reaction to an actual threat, but rather an attempt to activate a threat so that violence would erupt that would change the world. Propaganda is part of the action it is meant to justify."[11]

But it can also be argued that INFOOPS weighs against escalation. While a conflict remains a war of words, misinformation is abundant and the populace has difficulty discerning what's true and what's false. Perhaps a crisis will not erupt into all-out war — real or virtual.

Beyond INFOOPS lies the third, most alarming level of cyber conflict: attacks on critical infrastructure, public and private, with the goal of disrupting or disabling essential services. Escalation to this stage signals the formal onset of cyber war. The greater the real-world consequences of cyber attacks, the slipperier the slide, we believe, toward military hostilities — though by no well-understood, previously mapped route. The unpredictability of patterns wherein a conflict shifts from the virtual world to the real one is one probable, reassuring reason why cyber hostilities rarely ascend to this third level. Standing down would be difficult, justifying a conventional counterattack less so, even given the qualms harbored by the defenders of just war theory.

While the Ukraine crisis is used here as a repeated reference point, it would be wrong to conclude that international conflicts are the sole useful case studies for cyber theorists. Major political and cultural events—the Olympic Games, the Super Bowl, the World Cup, party and professional conventions, elections, New Year's Eve in Sydney or Times Square—are all potential cyber targets. All depend to some extent on digital information technology. Surely the Sochi Olympics were targeted—albeit apparently unsuccessfully—by cyber renegades seeking to score points of their own by destabilizing infrastructure. Surely, the intelligence services of other nations watched Sochi to learn about Russian cyber defenses.

What's the Answer? As we ascend

from one tier of cyber hostility to the next, the more urgent is the need for highly centralized command-and-control in government, simply because we have not observed, and do not yet comprehend, the unintended consequences of an all-out cyber conflict.

The uniquely fluid circumstances of cyber command demand strategies that abandon old conventions without divorcing cyber from other defense theaters. Computer scientist Robert F. Erbacher of Utah State University puts it well when he states: "[I]t is critical that cyber infrastructures and resources be incorporated into the command-and-control hierarchy. However, the significant differences in such a hierarchy require a distinct hierarchy, separate from the physical hierarchy. These two hierarchies must provide mechanisms for coordination due to their ability to impact one another."[12]

President Obama worries about unpredicted ripple effects from a cyber attack—the computerized equivalent of friendly fire.[13] Rightly so. An all-out cyber offensive could carom out of control in our interconnected world, and perhaps return to our own backyards. It could progress to a conventional attack as either a retaliatory or escalatory measure. For this reason alone, decisions to deploy cyber weapons should be made at the highest levels of government.

Rejoinders to first-level cyber hostilities, the "small attacks" that regularly pockmark computer defenses, will probably evolve toward automated responses. Dynamic, fast-moving conflicts may require faster action than humans can manage. Think of the relationship between a motorist and a vehicle's passive safety systems, from anti-lock brakes to lane-drift detectors: engineers design and iterate the technology, a driver may proactively activate it, but its effectiveness depends on automation. (No driver can pump the brakes as rapidly as a pulsing anti-lock mechanism.)

In the United States, command-and-control of second tier cyber conflicts—concentrated information operations—rests properly with MISO

Such authority must reside in the Oval Office, at least until greater experience reduces some of the uncertainties surrounding cyber warfare. We task the president with nuclear authority because we understand the awful consequences of a nuclear attack; with cyber offensive launch authority, it is because we don't know the consequences. Cyber weapons cannot be used cavalierly.

This approach to cyber command-

Borrowing from kinetic warfare's command-and-control playbook to wage this level of cyber conflict is probably fruitless, like trying to dispatch a swarm of hornets with a handgun.

(Military Information Support Operations), formerly known as PSYOP (Psychological Operations), whose broad brief is "to influence the perceptions, attitudes, and subsequent behavior of selected foreign audiences as part of approved MISO programs in support of USG policy and military objectives, plans, and operations."[14] Though clear political goals must be set at high levels, the decentralized tactical and operational command structure that has governed postwar campaigns of this nature remains appropriate. The unanswered questions are how hands-on MISO operatives will cope with new online and social media channels as they emerge, and whether INFOOPs should stick to deflating other states' propaganda or promoting its own.

Yet in third-tier cyber conflicts, where the intent is to disable an opponent's physical assets, a decentralized approach that pushes command authority down and into the field is ill advised.

and-control should be reinforced by international protocols that encourage data-sharing among like-minded nations and establishment of sanctions against non-state disruptors. It is optimistic to expect such actors to abide by treaties or conventions. But civilized nations can align against them with positive effect, as they have against terrorists in the 21st century. At any rate, the confidence of their citizens, and therefore their national security, depends on it.

The Price of Failure. The Internet runs on multilateral popular trust, which degrades when cyber hostilities excite international suspicions and counteractions. First-tier cyber attacks—data breaches, identity thefts, stolen property—can have a pernicious cumulative effect, driving one wary nation-state after another into a protective posture. Unless worldwide mutual defense strategies are defined

against non-state bad actors, we may observe the slow Balkanization of the Internet as governments prioritize local asset protection.

This trend is already occuring, inspired in part by fear of cyber hostilities. Survey data tells us that, thanks in part to "small" attacks on financial systems and retailers and rampant identity theft, the average citizen's trust in the Internet is decreasing steadily. Now, distrust is spreading to governments.

Germany claims to want an "Internet of its own," built to shield local traffic from snooping by foreign intelligence.[15] Brazil and Portugal are discussing building a private data link to bypass U.S.-based network access points.[16] As for international trade, U.S. technology companies are said to be suffering for the NSA's recently exposed surveillance activities: Forrester Research estimates the NSA developments mean up to $180 billion in lost business to U.S. firms through 2016.[17]

The open topography of the World Wide Web has heretofore defied the boundary-setting impulse typical of real-world human relations. We expect to show passports and use local currency when we visit other countries, and while traveling we scarcely expect to see television shows or favorite groceries from home. What if the Internet fractured along similar lines — with favorite websites, even email accounts, inaccessible from behind foreign borders? Will the United States be the first and last generation to know a barrier-free global Internet, blessedly unhampered by the visa checks and customs agents of the real world? Hopefully not. Yet fragmentation has begun.

We must make the hard choice to marshal a worldwide, organized response to cyber conflict that includes widely understood protocols for defense, command-and-control, and aid among allies. We must not shrink from the challenge. Avoidance means risking not only inadequate cyber defenses, but also degeneration of international trust and, faster than we might care to think, a fragmented Internet.

The course we choose, and the decisions we make about cooperation in cyberspace, will have far-reaching implications. We adopt digital technologies faster than we act to mitigate risks, including the risks of cyber hostilities.

It is to be hoped that as they flex and test their new capabilities, the world's fast multiplying cyber chessmasters, like the nuclear strategists of a prior age, are learning as they explore — particularly about the virtues of restraint. We may never be free of risks from cyber war, but we must quickly find ways to wage cyber peace as well.

NOTES

1 See https://www.ccdcoe.org. The Centre hosts a well-regarded annual conference on cyber security whose 2014 event was keynoted by the author.

2 Kertu Ruus, "Cyber War I: Estonia Attacked from Russia," The European Institute, Winter/Spring 2008: http://www.europeaninstitute.org/2007120267/Winter/Spring-2008/cyber-war-i-estonia-attacked-from-russia.html

3 "War in the Fifth Domain," *The Economist*, 1 July 2010 provides a helpful account of the genesis of Cybercom and similar commands.

4 Bill Gertz, "Washington Not Prepared for Cyber Warfare, Commander Warns," The Washington Times, 28 February 2014: http://www.washingtontimes.com/news/2014/feb/28/us-military-not-prepared-cyber-warfare-commander-w/#ixzz2zgcBkQBr

5 Jon Harper, "Wanted: Cyberwarriors, No Experience or Knowledge Necessary," Stars and Stripes, 29 March 2014: http://www.stripes.com/news/wanted-cyberwarriors-no-experience-or-knowledge-necessary-1.275172

6 Patrick Lin, Fritz Allhoff, and Neil Rowe, "Is it Possible to Wage a Just Cyberwar?" *The Atlantic*, 5 June, 2012. Lin is the director of the Ethics + Emerging Sciences Group in the philosophy department at California Polytechnic State University, San Luis Obispo. Allhoff is an associate philosophy professor at Western Michigan University and a senior research fellow at Australia's Centre for Applied Philosophy and Public Ethics. Rowe is a professor of computer science at the US Naval Postgraduate School. See http://www.theatlantic.com/technology/archive/2012/06/is-it-possible-to-wage-a-just-cyberwar/258106/ .

7 Mariarosaria Taddeo, University of Oxford University of Oxford blog on practical ethics, 6 June 2012: http://blog.practicalethics.ox.ac.uk/author/mariarosaria-taddeo/

8 During the Cold War the superpowers fought proxy conflicts, pouring training, money, and materiel into showdown theaters like Vietnam. Contract cyber warriors are the 21st century continuation of that practice, though of course one need no longer be a superpower to spark havoc.

9 Alan Yuhas, "Russian Propaganda Over Crimea and the Ukraine: How Does it Work?", *The Guardian*, 17 March 2014: http://www.theguardian.com/world/2014/mar/17/crimea-crisis-russia-propaganda-media

10 Timothy Snyder, "Crimea: Putin vs. Reality," New York Review of Books, NYR Blog, 7 March 2014: http://www.nybooks.com/blogs/nyrblog/2014/mar/07/crimea-putin-vs-reality/

11 Timothy Snyder, "Crimea: Putin vs. Reality," New York Review of Books, NYR Blog, 7 March 2014: http://www.nybooks.com/blogs/nyrblog/2014/mar/07/crimea-putin-vs-reality/

12 Robert F, Erbacher, "Extending Command and Control Infrastructures to Cyber Warfare Assets," Utah State University, 3 November 2010: CommandControl2.pdf

13 Josh Smith, "Obama Faces Delicate Decision as Cyberattack Fears Rise," *National Journal*, 23 August 2012: http://www.nationaljournal.com/tech/obama-faces-delicate-decision-as-cyberattack-fears-rise-20120823

14 Chairman of the Joint Chiefs of Staff Instruction 3110.05E, 30 September 2011. See https://publicintelligence.net/cjcs-miso/.

15 Leila Abboud and Peter Mauhagen, "Germany Wants a German Internet as Spying Scandal Rankles," Reuters, 25 October 2013: http://www.reuters.com/article/2013/10/25/us-usa-spying-germany-idUSBRE99O09S20131025

16 Nikolai Nielsen, "Brazil Champions Undersea Cable to Bypass US," EU Observer, 25 February 2014: http://euobserver.com/justice/123260

17 Jon Swartz, "NSA Surveillance Hurting Tech Firms' Businesses," USA TODAY, 28 February 2014: http://www.usatoday.com/story/tech/2014/02/27/nsa-resistant-products-obama-tech-companies-encryption-overseas/5290553/

The Hyper-Personalization of War

Cyber, Big Data, and the Changing Face of Conflict

Charles J. Dunlap, Jr.

"You may not be interested in war, but war is interested in you."
Leon Trotsky

For those who participate in it, all war can seem "hyper-personalized." But advances in cyber technology have enabled personalization to literally be taken to a whole new level, and this capability may make the role of cyber in future conflicts rather different than what is conceived today.

Popular conceptions of "cyber war" conjure up apocalyptic visions of aircraft crashing into each other due to disabled air traffic control systems, entire cities darkened as result of a computer breakdowns, and even nuclear plants melting down because of misdirected computerized instructions. These are the kind of incidents former Secretary of Defense Leon Panetta warned about in 2012 speech. According to Panetta, he feared a "cyber Pearl Harbor" that "would paralyze and shock the nation and create a new, profound sense of vulnerability. Likewise, President Obama characterized the cyber threat as "one of the most serious economic and national security challenges we face as a nation."[1]

Yet, increasing numbers of scholars are questioning that premise. In 2012, Professor Thomas Rid argued in an arti-

Maj. Gen. Charles J. Dunlap, Jr., USAF (Ret.) is Professor of Law at Duke University focusing on cyberwar, airpower, civil-military relations, and other issues related to national security and international law. Previously, he was a former deputy judge advocate general in the United States Air Force, and served 34 years in the Judge Advocate Corps.

cle entitled "Cyber War Will Not Take Place" that cyberwar has never happened, is not happening, and is "highly unlikely" to occur in the future.[2] Similarly, researchers Jerry Brito and Tate Watkins contended in 2012 that the evidence of an imminent cyber catastrophe is scant. While conceding that "cyberattacks and cyberespionage are real and serious concerns," that statement "is not evidence that we face a grave risk of national catastrophe."[3]

More recently, authors Bill Blunden and Violet Cheung claim in their new book, *Behold a Pale Farce: Cyber War, Threat Inflation, and That Malware Industrial Complex,* that the cyber threat has been overhyped for the purpose, they say, of making the public "so apprehensive and uneasy [about the cyber threat] they'll accept any solution to feel safe again."[4]

Less histrionically, the New York Times reports that prior to operations in Libya in 2010, the United States considered employing cyber methodologies against Gadhafi's military, but ultimately rejected it in part due to the sheer difficulty in doing so. The Times observed that although "popular fiction and films depict cyberattacks as easy to mount...in reality it takes significant digital snooping to identify potential entry points and susceptible nodes." Even then, writing and inserting the "proper poisonous codes" is challenging.[5]

This article suggests that our understanding of the potential permutations of cyber war may be incomplete. Assuming that cyber means will inexorably impact the characteristics of war in the 21st century, it argues that the growing capabilities of cyber methodologies may find a different application in

armed conflict than popularly assumed. In particular, "Big Data" technologies mainly intended for commercial uses enable not only the acquisition and archiving of vast amounts of data, but also empower a radically enhanced ability for rapid analysis. The convergence of these technologies will permit what might be called "the hyper-personalization of war."

The Technological Environment.

21st century conflicts will take place in an environment defined by enormous advances in information technologies. Though most realize that the number of people active in cyberspace has grown considerably, the actual figures can still be surprising.

For example, since the year 2000, the number of Internet users has grown 566%.[6] Significantly, this growth is not just in the developed world. The International Telecommunications Union (ITU) reports that by "the end of 2014, there will be almost 3 billion Internet users, with two-thirds of them coming from the developing world." Furthermore, ITU says "the number of mobile-broadband subscriptions will reach 2.3 billion globally," adding, "[f]ifty-five percent of these subscriptions are expected to be in the developing world."[7]

Equally important is the enormous amount of data available in cyberspace. In a 2012 estimate, "90% of the world's data was created in the last two years alone."[8] In fact, 2.5 quintillion bytes of data is created each day, which is "more data than was seen by everyone since the beginning of time."[9] Facebook users alone upload over 350 million images *per day*.[10]   As those millions of images indicate, there is a huge amount of personal information accessible online.

The loosely defined term for today's massive data sets is "Big Data."[11] Because of its potential to revolutionize how goods are sold, it is almost impossible to overstate the impact of the rise of "Big Data" on global commerce. Recognizing "Big Data's" potential to personalize marketing efforts to a truly unprecedented degree, businesses of all and social trending."[14] In other words, commercial entities can identify individuals or groups of individuals based on their behavior patterns gleaned from data in cyberspace.

The Weaponization of "Big Data".

Historically, developments in commerce and industry tend to make their way into the conduct of war. The availability of "Big Data" and the tools to analyze it present a real opportu-

It appears that in the not-too-distant future, the U.S. military will be able to launch swarms of drones of drones equipped with facial recognition software...

types are clamoring for a way to utilize it, and companies are responding. In the January 2014 issue of the *New York Review of Books*, Alice Marwick reports an entire "database marketing" industry has arisen that is devoted to "collecting, aggregating, and brokering personal data."[12] Marwick describes a firm that:

[C]reates profiles, or digital dossiers, about millions of people, based on the 1,500 points of data about them it claims to have. These data might include your education level; how many children you have; the type of car you drive; your stock portfolio; your recent purchases; and your race, age, and education level.

Such digital dossiers are sold to retailers who use the information to "hyper-personalize" their marketing efforts to specific consumers.[13] Some companies have used the "phenomenon of hyper-personalization" to categorize "users into neatly defined clusters based on their search history, buying behavior nity for governments to use "off-the-shelf technologies" to enhance their war fighting ability.

One obvious opportunity is to build databases of potential opponents' militaries that could be so detailed as to include electronic dossiers of individual members. The capability may already exist: according to press reports, the NSA collects millions of facial images each day for use in a sophisticated facial recognition program.[15] Consider the recent allegation that Chinese hackers stole thousands of personnel files on U.S. government workers.[16] Such information together with other data and technologies could be exploited during conflicts to personalize the means and methods of warfare to a wholly new degree.

It is critical to understand that cyber-derived data does not sit in isolation from other developing technologies. One technology that achieved significant prominence in recent years is the use of remotely-piloted aircraft commonly known as "drones" to engage in long-term surveillance of battlefields in Iraq, Afghanistan, and elsewhere, and to attack enemy fighters wherever found. Militaries around the world see the potential of these aircraft, and over the next decade spending on drones could top $89 billion worldwide.[17]

While issues exist regarding the current generation of drones' survivability against sophisticated opponents, there will no doubt be further improvements that could permit them to operate in contested air environments. Furthermore, published reports reveal that the U.S. military is developing a generation of small drones capable of operating in networked groups, or "swarms."[18] Other reports suggest efforts to develop lethal micro-drones that "resemble winged, multi-legged bugs" which "swarm through alleys, crawl across windowsills, and perch on power lines" as they seek their target.[19]

Parallel to the rapid development of drone technology is the swift advance of facial recognition software.[20] The linkage of the two in the context of "Big Data" was virtually inevitable. In 2013 the Associated Press, in a story provocatively entitled, "Drones With Facial Recognition Technology Will End Anonymity, Everywhere," explained that given the growing ubiquity of drones linked to massive databases:

> [C]yber experts believe it's only a matter of years — and research dollars — until computers can identify almost anyone instantly. Computers then could use electronic data to immediately construct an intimate dossier about the person, much of it from available information online

that many people put out there themselves.

The military sees the potential of these capabilities. *Popular Science* reports the U.S. Army is developing drones that can recognize people at a distance and in crowds.[21] The Army is also seeking to develop a "system [that] would integrate data from informants' tips, drone footage, and captured phone calls" so "a human behavior modeling and simulation engine" could spit out "intent-based threat assessments of individuals and groups."[22]

Warfighting Implications. What does this "cocktail" of cyber technologies mean for warfighting? Quite simply, it appears that in the not-too-distant future, the U.S. military - and likely other militaries - will be able to launch swarms of drones equipped with facial recognition software to roam battlefields looking for very specific members of an enemy's force. These could be officers, but also selected technicians and battle-hardened leaders who possess vital and difficult-to-replace skills.

Of course, militaries have long sought to 'decapitate' their enemies' forces. During the Revolutionary War, General Daniel Morgan, the commander of Morgan's Rifles (an elite group of sharpshooters) employed a "hyper-personalization" methodology that some considered "dishonorable."[23] Morgan and his unit "would hide and target British officers and Indian guides that the British sent out to scout out the land."[24] Although controversial, "it was effective" as it "would often send the British Army into chaos."[25] Sending an army into chaos though hyper-personalized attack is a valued capability in any era.

Drones are widely used today, but what is contemplated here is *swarms* of drones — hundreds, if not *thousands*. This would be a substantially more robust operation than the relatively modest, ongoing but limited effort to use drones to attack "senior operational terrorist leaders."[26] Nevertheless, it is instructive that the publicly available documents obtained from Osama bin Laden's compound during the raid that killed him express much concern about the damage done by drones. As one official put it, correspondence from an Al Qaeda field commander complained "that their guys were getting killed [by drones] faster than they could be replaced."[27]

What makes hyper-personalized war potentially so effective is not simply its ability to cripple military force by eliminating key personnel, but the *psychological* effect it could have on the force as a whole. One of the things that sustains soldiers in the crucible of combat is their relationship with others in their unit. This bonding process — the proverbial "band of brothers" — provides a shield against the psychological isolation of the battlefield. Otherwise, the extreme stress of combat can morph into fear, then panic, and even flight.

Hyper-personalized war alters this calculation by overtly targeting particular individuals; it makes it very clear that certain unit members — primarily the leadership cadre but also critical technicians and experts — are much more at risk than others. To some extent this is always been the case in war; however, the convergence of technologies in the 21st century accentuates and facilitates it in an unprecedented way.

Furthermore, history shows that certain weapons have tapped into primal human instincts in a way that conjures up a dislocating fear that is out of proportion to their actual effect. For example, the taboo regarding gas weapons seems to have originated in the "innate human aversion to poisonous substances."[28] Similarly, it might be said the hyper-personalization of war taps into the primal fear of being hunted.[29] This adds to the psychological disorientation that hyper-personalized war can inflict on modern armies.

Hyper-personalization of war also removes one of the chief "palliative techniques" that soldiers use to deal with combat stress: denial.[30] Essentially, the individual appreciates the danger of the situation but still believes that although others around him may become casualties, "the worst will never happen to [them]" personally.[31] Obviously, when an adversary has the ability to personalize the threat — and perhaps even communicate it directly — that fragile coping mechanism becomes inadequate.

The notion of wide scale - yet personal - contact with individuals of an opposing force is not without precedent. In fact, an early version of the hyper-personalization of war occurred before the start of the war against Iraq in 2003. U.S. forces dispatched thousands of personal e-mails to "Iraqi military officers warning them to abandon their positions and vehicles so not to suffer harm."[32]

Another opportunity to create psychological damage on an opponent's force was suggested in a 2001 article by Christopher C. Joyner and Catherine Lotrionte. They pointed out how terrorists and criminals could:

> "[D]ivert finds from bank computers and corrupt data in databases, causing disruption or panic" and "steal and disclose confidential personal, medical or financial information, as a tool of blackmail and extortion, and cause widespread social disruption or embarrassment."[33]

Today's "Big Data" capabilities would allow these examples to be converted into a means and method of warfare to be used not just by groups of terrorists and criminals, but also by armies in an effort to distract enemy troops from their war fighting focus. Such an operation could include, for example, widespread hacking of various cyberspace accounts of individual deployed soldiers and their families.

Knowing that an adversary could focus their efforts in such a personalized way could itself inflict psychological trauma.[34] Daniel Ventre records

lims achieved this effect by hacking email accounts, and by "intercepting cell phone calls between soldiers in Afghanistan and their families." It certainly seems possible that today a belligerent, and particularly one with state resources, could replicate this type of cyber-enabled — yet hyper-personalized - exploitation on a much wider scale.

Legal and Policy Implications.

Does the hyper-personalization of war offend legal or ethical regimes? The short answer seems to be, generally, "no". Developing a means to focus an attack on individual members of an enemy force is not unlawful; it is not, for example, an illegal form of assassination as many seem to believe.[36] In his 1989 U.S. Department of Defense memorandum about Executive Order 12333 (a Presidential directive about policies concerning intelligence activi-

What makes hyper-personalized war potentially so effective is not simply its ability to cripple military force by eliminating key personnel, but the psychological effect it could have on the force as a whole.

a 2007 incident in Denmark where "opponents of Western armed forces in their interventions" identified this vulnerability. He explained that Muslim extremists had "tried to intimidate families of Danish soldiers in Afghanistan" by contacting them directly. According to Ventre, this event "triggered a strong worry amongst the Danish."[35]

Ventre relates that the Mus-

ties, including assassination) Hays Parks, one of the nation's foremost experts on the law of armed conflict, detailed why killing individual enemy combatants in war is not "assassination" as understood in common parlance.[37]

Parks draws a sharp distinction between peacetime and wartime killings. "Peacetime assassination," he says, "would seem to encompass the murder of a private individual or public figure for political purposes" something international law prohibits irrespective of an Executive

vidualized attack on the same basis as members of traditional, uniformed militaries, as long as they perform a "continuous combat function."[41]

Of course, international law pro-

Hacking a civilian's e-mail system during armed conflict to direct a propaganda e-mail personally to him or her does not violate the law of war...

Order.[38] However, the killing of combatants in war is a very different matter. Parks points out that as a matter of international law "the role of the military [in wartime] includes legalized killing" and that combatants "are liable to attack at any time or place."[39]

An individual combatant's "vulnerability to lawful targeting," Parks observes, "is not dependent upon his or her 'military duties, or proximity to combat as such'."[40] Furthermore, any lawful weapon or technique can be used. Parks cites a number of historical examples, including the 1943 downing of a Japanese aircraft carrying Admiral Yamamoto Isoroku. Accordingly, a cyber-empowered technique that permits hyper-personalization of war could be lawfully employed against individual belligerents.

Furthermore, the consensus among international lawyers is that non-state actors in a bona fide armed conflict who organize themselves into armed groups engaged in continuous combat operations against other similar armed groups or nation-states are subject to indi-

hibits making targets of civilians not directly involved in hostilities. Protocol I to the Geneva Conventions calls upon the parties to distinguish "between the civilian population and combatants in between civilian objects and military objectives."[42] Protocol I further directs the parties to a conflict "shall direct operations only against military objectives."[43]

Consequently, civilians "enjoy general protection against dangers arising from military operations."[44] Additionally, international law provides that "acts or threats of violence the primary purpose of which is to spread terror among civilian population are prohibited." However, this prohibition does not exempt civilians from *all* consequences of war.

For example, international law only considers "attacks" as cyber operations that are "violent" - that is, designed to cause death, injury or significant damage.[45] A cyber-operation that is purely *psychological* in nature — such as propaganda - may 'target' civilians so long as it does not aim to "incite the population to commit crimes."[46]

Along these lines, hacking a civilian's e-mail system during armed conflict to direct a propaganda e-mail personally to him or her does not violate the law of war (although it may violate domestic law).[47] Even if a personalized email threatens to target a son or daughter who is serving in the armed forces unless the family fails to take steps to actively oppose the war, it is unlikely that such action would violate international law. It is permissible to attack or threaten to attack a bona fide combatant as, presumably, the actively deployed military family member would be.

In contrast, an email that threatened an action violating the law of war would indeed violate international law. For example, it would be unlawful to threaten to kill or kidnap a civilian family member not directly participating in hostilities. Furthermore, international law prohibits targeting a civilian object not being used for military purposes.[48]

This would mean that a cyber "operation" (as the term is used in Protocol I) designed to hack into a civilian's personal bank account or medical records (as Joyner's and Lotrionte' article hypothesizes criminals or terrorists might do) would be illegal under international law. Indeed, targeting the personal property of a *combatant* is likewise typically a breach of the law because it is not necessarily part of a proper military objective.

Conclusion.
The emergence of cyber-enabled "hyper-personalized" war raises a variety of issues for 21st century democracies. For instance,

what effect will it have on military recruitment and retention, particularly in the growing number of countries like the US that rely on all-volunteer militaries? Adversaries' abilities to literally "reach out and touch" particular individuals could adversely affect the mindsets of individuals who otherwise would be disposed to serve in the military, as well as "influencers" of military service, such as parents, spouses, and friends.[49]

Moreover, there are a nearly endless number of scenarios where adversaries could hyper-personalize conflict via cyber means. Enemy agents could track the online habits, school schedules, and other activities of servicemembers' children and employ data-mining and other cyber-techniques to pinpoint them. This information could then be used to plot all kinds of actual malevolence against their children, or to simply craft very precise threats toward their families. In either case, enormous anxiety would be generated among the troops about the safety of their loved ones. It would make it almost impossible for soldiers to focus on warfighting duties.

This scenario also shows that the hyper-personalization of war, particularly through the exploitation of open-source information, may disadvantage democracies and other open societies simply because it would be easier to build the database of targets. While it is probable that even the relatively few remaining truly closed societies (like North Korea) will eventually be obliged to provide their peoples with access to the Internet, it is readily conceivable that freer societies where individuals are almost fully unconstrained about the sharing of personal information would obviously be more vulnerable.

Another dark side of the hyper-personalization of war is that the cyber technologies that enable it are not especially unique to the United States or other advanced democracies. In most instances, they are available on the commercial market. In the hands of the totalitarian or repressive regimes - something that is virtually inevitable — these capabilities would facilitate the identification and elimination of dissidents.

At the same time, combatants waging hyper-personalized war who also observe the law could aid in shielding innocents from the consequences of conflict. Not only might the application of force be limited to bona fide belligerents, even within that group only a select few might need to be targeted. Narrowing the number of combatants at risk, and limiting (or even eliminating) many of the dangers to civilians might ameliorate some of the horror of war. Recently, the Israelis illustrated another risk-limiting hyper-personalization technique when they called the personal cell phones of Gaza civilians to warn them that the building they were occupying was about to be bombed.[50]

Finally, it cannot be over-emphasized that hyper-personalized war is not necessarily the only, or even most likely, form of "cyberwar" that we could see in the 21st century. Still, acknowledging and preparing for the inventive application of cyber capabilities occasioned by the rise of "Big Data" and all that comes with it is vital. Absent doing so, we may find ourselves suffering not the "cyber Pearl Harbor" that Mr. Panetta fears, but another one with consequences equally as serious consequences.

NOTES

1 President Barak Obama, "Remarks by the President on Securing Our Nation's Cyber the Structure" (Washington, DC, 29 May 2009).

2 Thomas Rid, "Cyber Will Not Take Place," *Journal of Strategic Studies* 35 (February 2012): 6.

3 Jerry Brito and Tate Watkins, "Cyberwar Is the New Yellowcake," Wired, February 14, 2012 http://www.wired.com/2012/02/yellowcake-and-cyberwar/ (accessed 29 June 2014).

4 Bill Blunden and Violet Cheung, *Behold a Pale Farce: Cyber War, Threat Inflation, and That Malware Industrial Complex* (Walterville, OR: Trine Day, 2014) 9.

5 Eric Schmitt and Thom Shanker, "U.S. Debated Cyberwarfare in Attack Plan on Libya." *New York Times*, 17 October 2011.

6 "World Internet Usage and Population Statistics," Internet World Stats, http://www.internetworldstats.com/stats.htm (accessed 29 June 2014).

7 Brahima Sanou, "The World in 2014: ICT Facts and Figures," http://www.itu.int/en/ITU-D/Statistics/Documents/facts/ICTFactsFigures2014-e.pdf (accessed 29 June 2014).

8 "How Much Data is on the Internet and Generated Online Every Minute?," Internet, http://removeandreplace.com/2013/03/13/how-much-data-is-on-the-internet-and-generated-online-every-minute/ (accessed 29 June 2014).

9 Ibid.

10 Cooper Smith, "Facebook Users Are Uploading 350 Million New Photos Each Day," *Business Insider*, September. 18, 2013, http://www.businessinsider.com/facebook-350-million-photos-each-day-2013-9#ixzz350CnZqkK (accessed 18 June 2014).

11 Uri Friedman, "Big Data: A Short History," *Foreign Policy*, http://www.foreignpolicy.com/articles/2012/10/08/big_data (accessed 29 June 2014).

12 Alice E. Marwick, "How Your Data Are Being Deeply Mined," *New York Review of Books* 61, no. 1 (9 January 2014).

13 Rachel Strugatz, "Digital's Next Wave: Hyper-Personalization," *WWD* (15 April 2013) http://www.wwd.com/retail-news/marketing-consumer-behavior/digitals-next-wave-hyper-personalization-6892657 (accessed 29 June 2014).

14 Ibid.

15 Dana Ford, *Report: NSA collects millions of facial images per day*, CNN, 2 June 2014, http://www.cnn.com/2014/06/01/politics/nsa-facial-recognition/ (accessed 29 June 2014).

16 Michael S. Schmidt, David E. Sanger, and Nicole Perloth, "Chinese Hackers Pursue Key Data on U.S. Workers," New York Times, July 9, 2014, http://www.nytimes.com/2014/07/10/world/asia/chinese-hackers-pursue-key-data-on-us-workers.html (accessed 10 July 2014).

17 *Teal Group Predicts Worldwide UAV Market Will Total $89 Billion in Its 2013 UAV Market Profile and Forecast*, Teal Group, June 17, 2013, http://tealgroup.com/index.php/about-teal-group-corporation/press-releases/94-2013-uav-press-release (accessed 30 June 2014).

18 Debra Warner, *Drone Swarm: Networks of Small UAVs Offer Big Capabilities*, Defense News, June 12, 2013, http://www.defensenews.com/article/20130612/C4ISR/306120029/Drone-Swarm-Networks-Small-UAVs-Offer-Big-Capabilities (accessed 30 June 2014).

19 http://www.theatlantic.com/technology/archive/2013/02/like-a-swarm-of-lethal-bugs-the-most-terrifying-drone-video-yet/273270/ (accessed 30 June 2014).

20 Facial recognition software is:
> [A]n application that can be used to automatically identify or verify individuals from video frame or digital images. Some facial recognition software uses algorithms that analyze specific facial features, such as the relative position, size and shape of a person's nose, eyes, jaw and cheekbones.

"Facial Recognition Software," Tecopedia, http://www.techopedia.com/definition/26948/facial-recognition-software (accessed 30 June 2014).

21 Noah Shachtman, "Army Tracking Plan: Drones That Never Forget a Face," Wired, September 28, 2011, http://www.wired.com/2011/09/drones-never-forget-a-face/ (accessed 30 June 2014).

22 Ibid.

23 "Daniel Morgan," The History Junkie, http://thehistoryjunkie.com/daniel-morgan/ (accessed 29 June 2014).

24 Ibid.

25 Ibid.

26 White House, "Fact Sheet: US Policy Standards and Procedures for Use of Force in Counterterrorism Operations outside the United States and Areas of Active Hostilities," May 23, 2013, http://www.whitehouse.gov/the-press-office/2013/05/23/fact-sheet-us-policy-standards-and-procedures-use-force-counterterrorism (accessed 30 June 2014).

27 Greg Miller, *Bin Laden document trove shows strain on Al Qaeda*, Washington Post, http://www.washingtonpost.com/national/national-security/bin-laden-document-trove-reveals-strain-on-al-qaeda/2011/07/01/AGdj0GuH_story_1.html (accessed 30 June 2014).

28 Harold Maas, *A Brief History of Chemical Warfare*, The Week, September 7, 2013, http://shawnelliott.blogspot.com/2009/03/primal-fear-haunted-by-ghosts-of.html (accessed 30 June 2014).

29 Shawn Elliot, *Primal Fear: Haunted by Ghosts of Predators Past*, March 22, 2009, http://shawnelliott.blogspot.com/2009/03/primal-fear-haunted-by-ghosts-of.html (accessed 30 June 2014).

30 Richard Holmes, *Acts of War: the Behavior of Men in Battle* (New York: The Free Press, 1985) 233.

31 Ibid.

32 Roscini, 240.

33 Christopher C. Joyner and Catherine Lotri-

NOTES

onte, "Information Warfare as International Core-cion: A Legal Framework," 12 European Journal of International Law 838 (2001).

34 Daniel Ventre, *Cyber War and Information Warfare* (London: Wiley, 2011) 75.

35 Ibid.

36 See e.g., Bill Quigley, http://www.informationclearinghouse.info/article31330.htm

37 W. Hays Parks,"Executive Order 12333 and Assassination," (US Department of Defense, 2 November 1989), https://www.law.upenn.edu/institutes/cerl/conferences/targetedkilling/papers/Parks-Memorandum.pdf (accessed 29 June 2014).

38 Ibid.

39 Ibid.

40 Ibid.

41 *Tallinn Manual on the International Law Applicable to Cyber Warfare* (Cambridge: Cambridge Univ: Press, 2013) 116.

42 International Committee of the Red Cross (ICRC), *Protocol Additional to the Geneva Conventions of 12 August 1949, and relating to the Protection of Victims of International Armed Conflicts (Protocol I)*, 8 June 1977, 1125 UNTS 3, art. 48, available at: http://www.refworld.org/docid/3ae6b36b4.html (accessed 29 June 2014). Although The United States Is not a party to Protocol

I, most scholars consider this portion to be part of customary international law applicable to all nations.

43 Protocol I, art. 52 defines military objectives as "those objects which by their nature, location, purpose or use make an effective contribution to military action and whose total or partial destruction, capture or neutralization, in the circumstances ruling at the time, offers a definite military advantage."

44 Protocol I, art 51.

45 William H. Boothby, *The Law of Targeting* (Oxford: Oxford Univ. Press, 2012) 387.

46 Marco Roscini, *Cyber Operations and the Use of Force in International Law* (Oxford: Oxford Univ. Press, 2014), 241.

47 Boothby, 398.

48 *Tallinn Manual*, Rule 38, 125-135.

49 Donna Miles, "Army Recruiting Campaign Focuses on Prospects, Influencers," 30 August 2005, http://www.defense.gov/news/newsarticle. aspx?id=16767 (accessed 30 June 2014).

50 Steven Erlanger and Fares Akram, "Israel Warns Gaza Targets by Phone and Leaflet," New York Times, July 9, 2014, http://www.nytimes.com/2014/07/09/world/middleeast/by-phone-and-leaflet-israeli-attackers-warn-gazans.html?_r=0 (accessed 10 July 2014).

Inverted-Militarized-Diplomacy

How States Bargain with Cyber Weapons

Richard B. Andres

While a great deal of work examines how states use conventional and nuclear weapons in militarized interstate bargaining, little work has examined how states bargain with cyber weapons to further their national interests. The few authors who take on this question conclude that it is difficult or even impossible to bargain with weapons that work best when they are secret and not attributable. This approach is mistaken. With cyber weapons, states regularly employ an inverted militarized bargaining method in which, rather than making demands backed by threats, policymakers use military assets to seize what they want while relying on diplomats to prevent reprisal and escalation.

In recent years, militaries have increased their spending on cyber weapons and become more active in placing offensive malware in their adversaries' systems. As these capabilities have proliferated, leaders from various countries have warned that cyber warfare can now cause harm on par with conventional weapons.[1] Nevertheless, the increase in the military use of the cyber domain has not been accompanied by much academic discussion about the diplomatic bargaining strategies that accompany these armaments.[2]

Part of the problem scholars have with writing about

Richard B. Andres is Professor of National Security Strategy at the U.S. National War College, focusing on cyber, aerospace, and energy. Previously, he was Special Advisor to the Secretary of the Air Force and has led teams developing strategy for the White House, Chief of Staff of the Air Force, Commandant of the Marine Corps, Office of the Secretary of Defense, and other combatant commands.

cyber strategy is that cyber diplomacy does not fit well into existing models of militarized bargaining. Standard bargaining models of war posit that states deploy weapons in order to increase their diplomatic leverage over other states.[3] National leaders display their military capabilities to deter or compel their adversaries. Unlike most conventional arms, however, cyber weapons often become less operationally effective when they cease to be secret and when they can be attributed to a specific attacker. Thus the paradox: when a state

The current theoretical understanding of cyber diplomacy is unsatisfying. The argument that secret and anonymous weapons cannot be used to achieve political goals is inaccurate. States regularly use secret and anonymous military power in conjunction with diplomacy using a technique I term *inverted militarized diplomacy*, in which states use plausibly deniable military power to seize desired goods while using diplomacy to prevent retaliation and escalation. Historically, this method has been used most often by nations employing pirates against

Using inverted militarized diplomacy, states use plausibly deniable military power to seize desired goods while using diplomacy to prevent retaliation and escalation.

makes its cyber threats transparent in order to advance diplomatic ends, it renders its cyber capabilities less operationally potent and thus diplomatically less useful. In short, diplomatic threats that reveal cyber weapons tend to nullify themselves.[4]

The main way the international relations literature has addressed this problem is to avoid it. Eric Gartzke writes that cyberwar is a myth; policymakers have exaggerated the threat.[5] Thomas Rid argues that the requirement for secrecy and anonymity prevents policymakers from using cyber weapons as tools of policy.[6] Martin Libicki goes further, arguing that the fact that cyber weapons rely on deception makes it difficult to even theorize about how they might mesh with nations' grand strategic goals.[7]

adversaries' commerce or fomenting rebellion in opponents' populations. Today, inverted militarized diplomacy is central to the three main methods states use to employ cyber weapons against each other. Over the last few years, the cyber strategies major powers have utilized have had a significant effect on global economics, politics and balances of power.

Weapons Technology and Inverted Militarized Diplomacy.

Over the last few decades, a good deal of work has explored how states use weapons to bargain. In the simplest model of bargaining, when an initiator desires a good held by a target, it makes a demand backed by the threat of force. When a target receives the demand, it must decide whether to resist or comply. If it resists, the initiator must choose whether to go through with the threat. When the target believes the initiator's threat is credible and that it can impose costs greater than the cost of losing the disputed good, it will concede. If the target believes the threat is a bluff or that the initiator does not have sufficient military capacity to impose costs greater than the value of the disputed good, it will resist.[8]

An interesting line of research into militarized diplomacy involves weapons technology and tactics. A highly scrutinized phenomenon involves the difference between bargaining with conventional and nuclear weapons. For states bargaining with conventional weapons, the classic problem involves how to make threats credible, since both states have incentives to exaggerate the strengths of their military power. The traditional solution is to publically display capabilities either statically or on the battlefield in limited wars. While talk is cheap, displays are harder to misrepresent. When states make demands backed by conventional weapons, the threats generally must be attributable and there is an incentive to display the military capabilities that is being used to carry out both deterrent and compellent threats.[9]

There are substantial similarities between the way states bargain with conventional and nuclear weapons. There is, however, an important difference. In nuclear bargaining, the threat of escalation to general war is inherently incredible since both actors know that the costs of such a war would eclipse whatever gains an initiator might gain by winning. In this type of bargaining, once both states have the ability to destroy the other, their relative capacity becomes largely unimportant. This significantly reduces states' incentive to statically display their nuclear capacity and particularly to display it in combat. In this situation, the diplomatic task becomes one of displaying risk acceptance rather than military power. A state with hundreds of weapons and a reputation for irrationality would likely have a bargaining advantage over a state with thousands of weapons but a reputation for reasonableness. To overcome this problem, states attempt to build artificial irrationality into their bureaucratic systems and otherwise increase their opponents' perception that they are willing to use nuclear weapons under specific circumstances. States employ tripwire deployments of troops, hair-trigger forces, autonomous battlefield nuclear weapons and other schemes to increase the chances that a state would use nuclear weapons even when doing so might lead to general war and mutually assured destruction.[10]

While diplomacy involving conventional and nuclear weapons relies on overt displays and attributable threats, there are classes of weapons and tactics that work best when this process is inverted; however, this type of militarized bargaining has received little attention in the bargaining literature. In inverted militarized diplomacy, the initiator begins an interaction with a target by using its military capability to seize what it wants by force and fraud rather than by demanding that the target concede the good. This technique puts the target in a position where it must either escalate or accept the new status quo. In this type of scenario, the initiator's diplomatic goal is to prevent escalation and reprisal. This approach differs from a simple fait accompli strategy in that it can describe persistent military operations that are occurring coeval to diplomatic activity and can be expected to continue into the future. It differs from a brute force strategy in that the initiator does not forgo diplomacy; rather it uses diplomacy to prevent the target from retaliating. Traditionally, diplomats use this strategy to lower the chances of reprisal by lowering the target's expectations about the utility of retaliation and escalation. This often involves efforts to decrease the target's certainty about the identity of the attacker, to lower the target's estimation of the value of the thing being purloined, or to increase the target's assessment of the cost of escalation.

For practical reasons, some types of weapons and tactics facilitate inverted militarized diplomacy and some do not; four characteristics tend to increase the utility of a military technology for this purpose. First, technology and techniques that allow military force to be used without attribution (or at least provide plausible deniability) increase its utility. Second, methods that permit forces to seize goods with high political or economic value make the approach more attractive. Third, less socially provocative weapons and tactics are more conducive to the inverted bargaining approach; for instance, if a state fired a cruise missile to destroy a factory, most observers would consider the act more provocative than if the state employed a computer virus to accomplish the same end.[11] Finally, the approach works best when the initiator

perceives an asymmetrical opportunity to use force; that is, when the initiator has the opportunity to take something from the target by force but the target cannot easily respond in kind. Across history, the utility of the inverted approach has waxed and waned with the rise and fall of various types of military and economic technology and changing perceptions about the meaning of different types of military action.[12]

While there are many examples of technologies and tactics that states have used with inverted militarized diplomacy, the two best known examples are state-sponsored piracy and state-promoted insurgency. How effective these methods are depends, to a large extent, on the technology of the day. In the sixteenth century, Elizabeth I of England sponsored pirates to attack Spanish shipping. The stratagem was attractive because the maritime and financial technology of day enabled un-attributable pirate ships to steal vast sums in bullion (enriching sponsoring states and weakening rivals) and because pirate-states could act without positive attribution. In this interaction, Spain could not retaliate in kind because England did not have similarly exposed supply lines (vulnerable treasure convoys from the New World). Through astute diplomacy, Elizabeth was able to defer conventional retaliation for decades.[13]

States have also used inverted militarized diplomacy to foment insurgency in opponents' populations. One of the best known examples involves the Cold War interaction between the United States and the Soviet Union and their client states. During the early years of the Cold War, the Soviet Union regularly supported violent people's movements in non-communist nations. The strategy was effective because of a confluence of technologies and social conditions. Originally, the strategy was attractive because it did not appear that the United States could respond in kind. The Soviet Union depended on a combination of secrecy, plausible deniability, and playing with nuclear thresholds to prevent the United States from escalating. The strategy eventually lost its value when, in the 1980s, the United States began promoting anti-communist insurgencies in Nicaragua and Afghanistan, and successful dissident movements in other countries, including the Soviet Union itself.

Cyber weapons and militarized diplomacy.
In the cyber age, states are maneuvering to find ways to use weaponized software to further national interests. So far, the half dozen or so cyber-powers have gravitated toward three main strategic activities: piracy of intellectual property, fomenting of revolution, and sabotage of critical infrastructure. Each of these approaches relies on a combination of secrecy, disguised attribution, and inverted diplomacy.

Piracy of intellectual property.
The first way states utilize cyber weapons as tools of policy involves piracy of intellectual property (IP). Throughout history, international law and custom governing espionage have been ambiguous. For the most part, the law remains silent concerning the theft of state secrets. This norm has evolved for a number of technical and practical reasons. Notably, espionage often helps

both the spying and spied-on nations. Inaccurate information is one of the most common causes of war. Bilateral espionage can reduce the chances violence. Similarly, IP piracy is seldom considered as serious as stealing tangible goods. In countries such as China, there is not a strong norm against it. Beyond these issues, the harm spying can do has traditionally been reduced by the cost of placing spies and their limited ability to exfiltrate information. Thus, while states regularly complain about foreign spies operating on their soil, these protests seldom amount to casus billis.

The problem with new cyber espionage technology is that it radically changes the cost-benefit tradeoff for spying. While placing a human agent often requires large investments for small rewards, cyber spying costs little and regularly produces massive payoffs. By conservative estimates, IP theft costs the United States around 375 billion dollars each year, around 2 million jobs, with China responsible for most of the loss.[14]

The dynamics of cyber IP piracy are similar to those of high seas piracy during the Elizabethan period. Over the last two decades, the developed world, and the United States in particular, has increasingly outsourced its production of physical goods to Asia, turning to a business model based on developing IP. As the value of IP has burgeoned, pirate-states, and China in particular, have used their militaries' cyber resources to steal it. The dilemma for IP-producing nations is much the same as that faced by sixteenth century Spain: the states doing most of the pirating do not have much that can be pirated in retaliation. Diplomatically, the cyber pirate-states face the same challenge as Elizabeth. The sums being won and lost through piracy rise to the level of national policy and, at least in the case of China, are helping to change regional balances of economic and military power toward the pirate-states.[15] Pirate-states attempt to prevent retaliation and escalation through secrecy, misinformation, plausible denial, and other diplomatic means.[16] The main risk their leaders face is that, like Elizabeth, they will eventually misjudge Western thresholds for reprisal in a game with which neither side has much experience.[17]

Fomenting Revolution.

A second way states use cyber weapons as tools of policy involves encouraging revolution. Like espionage, external support for dissidents has traditionally inhabited a gray area in international law and custom. States encouraging revolutions often see their actions not only as politically useful, but as morally right. This was certainly the case with republican France, Soviet communism, and modern liberal democracy.

For the last few years, Western states, and particularly the United States, have used cyber tools to undermine repressive autocratic regimes. Most policymakers in democratic states probably do not see these actions as fomenting rebellions so much as supporting freedom. In a landmark speech in 2010 Secretary of State Hillary Clinton laid out U.S. cyber policy as morally obliged to break down the information barriers autocratic regimes erect against cyber freedom.[18] Congress has funded this mission and various U.S. departments

and agencies have supported it by developing and distributing anonymizing software designed to allow dissidents in autocratic countries to communicate and coordinate their actions.[19] Western-supplied social media, anonymizing software, and virtual private networks (VPN) have contributed to movements that have overthrown regimes in Tunisia, Egypt (twice), Libya, and Ukraine and threatened governments in Iran, Syria, Yemen, Bahrain, and Iraq.[20] Russia and China have both regularly declared the U.S. cyber openness efforts to be recklessly offensive and, China in particular, has spent vast sums developing the so called Great Firewall of China to prevent dissidents from coordinating via electronic means. China has reason to worry as it has spent almost as many years in civil war as not over past two centuries and its civil wars have often cost it millions of lives.

From the perspective of international relations and diplomacy, the dynamics behind current Western efforts to use cyber tools to help dissidents coordinate their actions are similar to the early twentieth century attempts by the Soviet Union to encourage revolution. The West and the United States in particular, has been able to pursue this policy with impunity because democracies appear to be immune to the negative effects that this technology poses for regime stability and, consequently, its autocratic rivals cannot retaliate in kind. The diplomatic goal of the West is to prevent escalation and retaliation by other means. It does this by playing up the moral imperative behind freedom of information and playing down its own role in providing software, which is easily done because private groups take on this role without need for encouragement. For their part, repressive states seek to blame Western powers for their dissident movements while seeking treaties that limit Western action on their networks.[21] The main risk the West faces by promoting this policy is that it will work. For instance, the current Western supported civil war in Syria weakened the regime and thereby helped a rebel army, the Islamic State in Iraq and Syria (ISIS) to mobilize, invade and conquer a large part of U.S. supported Iraq; the Western friendly coup that displaced the Russian friendly government in Ukraine motivated Russia to invade Crimea and Eastern Ukraine with irregular forces. A revolution or coup in Russia or China has the potential to lead to unintended consequences such as global financial turmoil or loose nuclear weapons.

Critical infrastructure sabotage.

A third way states are employing cyber weapons involves sabotaging opponents' critical infrastructure. Over the last four years, U.S. Directors of National Intelligence have repeatedly described this as the foremost item in their annual threat assessments to the Senate.[22] These types of attacks are sometimes described as capable of creating a Cyber Pearl Harbor. Just as Russian and Chinese leaders describe fomenting rebellion in their populations as their greatest fear, U.S. leaders describe critical infrastructure sabotage as theirs.[23]

While this type of malware can threaten military systems and various types of civilian infrastructure, the greatest threat it possesses is to national electrical grids because all other critical infrastructures depend on electricity.[24] In many countries, including the United States, electric grids are old, complex, and fragile. The industrial control systems (ICS) and supervisory control and data acquisition (SCADA) infrastructure that controls most grids globally are poorly protected and difficult to defend. Against a country like the United States, a military launching a full scale attack on an electric grid would most likely use malware to attempt to destroy hardware such as ultrahigh voltage transformers and large generators that require months or years to replace. While it would be difficult to accomplish, a fully successful attack could result in millions of deaths and national economic paralysis.[25] A state might be willing to launch this type of attack if it believed it had no other options; for instance, if its regime were about to fall to conventional attack. A state might also launch a smaller attack with the goal of causing economic loss and military debilitation. Attackers might see this second type of action as operating below the threshold

The dilemma for [intellectual property]-producing nations is much the same as that faced by sixteenth century Spain: the states doing most of the pirating do not have much that can be pirated in retaliation.

that would invite massive retaliation by its opponent's military.[26] Over the last year, a large proportion of electric companies around the globe have reported finding malware in the systems that control their hardware.[27]

Critical infrastructure sabotage has asymmetrical political value in that prevent reprisal. Beyond this, a key element that makes this bargaining strategy successful involves social conventions about cyberspace; if opponents buried physical bombs under transformers and generators it is more likely that populations and policymakers would feel compelled to retaliate.

[Sabotaging critical infrastructure] is risky but a number of states appear to believe the potential it offers to gain global power projection capability on the cheap is worth the risk.

developed economies are often more dependent on critical infrastructure than less developed states. When the power goes out in most rich countries, within seconds economic transactions and communication stop working and within hours electricity dependent water and fuel stop flowing. Developing nations tend to be less dependent on electricity. More importantly, though, this type of weapon is a way for states without global power projection capability to harm their distant opponents without spending trillions of dollars on bases, bombers, and aircraft carriers.

Like the methods of cyber-attack described earlier, critical infrastructure sabotage employs a form of inverted diplomacy. States that place malware on opponents' systems without activating it do so to increase their military power. Rather than making diplomatic demands backed by cyber-weapons, their militaries emplace their weapons in their opponents' territory by stealth and fraud. Diplomatically, attackers rely on a combination of secrecy, plausible deniability and lack of precedent to

The sabotage strategy carries a number of difficulties and risks. These weapons and techniques are challenging to develop; conducting the kind of virtual Pearl Harbor U.S. policymakers warn about would be tough. Even if a state had the capability, the weapons would be unreliable because an attacker would not know if the defender had neutralized the malware in the months or years it lay dormant waiting for the signal to detonate.[28] Moreover, sending potentially devastating malware into the wild is dangerous both because discovered-malware can be reverse engineered and because of the possibility that malware resident on critical infrastructure might detonate through error or accident.[29] In short, this approach is risky but a number of states appear to believe the potential it offers to gain global power projection capability on the cheap is worth the risk.

Conclusion. The above analysis described the logic behind the three main ways states are using offensive cyber weapons. States use these arms to achieve political objectives by force and fraud, and then use diplomatic efforts to prevent retaliation and escalation. This reverses the model political scientists are accustomed to, in which militarized interactions begin with diplomats making threats about the potential future use of force. The literature is mistaken in arguing that states cannot utilize cyber weapons as tools of policy. Just as nuclear weapons require bargaining strategies somewhat different from conventional weapons, cyber weapons require an approach somewhat different from either conventional or nuclear diplomacy. Policymakers and generals around the world are using this model to achieve their foreign policy objectives.

NOTES

1 Alexei Nokolski, "Putin Urges Readiness Against Cyber and Outer Space Attacks," RIA Novosti, 5 July 2013. On the US side see, Elisabeth Bumiller and Thom Shanker, "Panetta Warns of Dire Threat of Cyberattack," New York Times, 11 October 2012.

2 Lucas Kello, "The Meaning of the Cyber Revolution: Perils to Theory and Statecraft." International Security 38, no.2 (Fall 2013): 7-40, particularly 1-2.

3 The literature on militarized interstate bargaining is one of the most prolific in the field of international relations. For an overview see Dan Reiter, "Exploring the Bargaining Model of War." Perspective on Politics 1, no. 1 (March 2003): 27-43.

4 See for instance Ryan Grauer, "Old Wine in New Bottles: The Nature of Conflict in the 21st Century," The Whitehead Journal of Diplomacy and International Relations 14, no. 1 (Winter/Spring 2013): 9-22.

5 Erik Gartzke, "The Myth of Cyberwar: Bringing War in Cyberspace Back Down to Earth," International Security 38, no. 2 (Fall 2013): 41-73.

6 Thomas Rid, "Cyberwar and Peace: Hacking Can Reduce Real-World Violence." Foreign Affairs 92, no. 6 (November-December 2013): 77-87, particularly 77-78.

7 Martin Libicki. "Why Cyber War Will Not and Should Not Have Its Grand Strategist." Strategic Studies Quarterly 8, no. 1 (Spring 2014): 23-39, particularly 33.

8 For early models of his type see for instance, Bruce Mesquita, The War Trap (New Haven: Yale University Press, 1981; Bruce Mesquita and David Lalman, War and Reason: Domestic and International Imperatives (New Haven: Yale University Press, 1992). For and overview of bargaining theory, see Dan Reiter, "Exploring the Bargaining Model of War," Perspective on Politics 1, no. 1 (2003): 27-43.

9 The classical work on this is Geoffrey Blainey, The Causes of War (New York: Free Press, 1973). On costly signals see J. D Fearon, "Signaling Versus the Balance of Power and Interests: An Empirical Test of a Crisis Bargaining Model," Journal of Conflict Resolution 38, no. 2 (1994): 236-269.

10 Thomas C. Schelling, Arms and influence (New Haven: Yale University Press, 1966). Albert Wohlstetter, "The Delicate Balance of Terror," Foreign Affairs 37, no. 2 (January 1959): 211–34. For the classical game theoretic analysis, see Robert Powell, Nuclear Deterrence Theory: The Search for Credibility (Cambridge: Cambridge University Press, 2008).

11 For the seminal discussion on social construction as it relates to ways of using force see Thomas C. Schelling, Arms and influence (New Haven: Yale University Press, 1966), particularly chapter 4.

12 On how changes in military technology affect incentives, see Emily O. Goldman and Richard B. Andres, "Systemic Effects of Military Innovation and Diffusion," Security Studies 8, no. 4 (1999): 79-125. For case studies of how modern precision weapons technology lowers the impetus for reprisal see: Richard B. Andres, Craig Wills, and Thomas E. Griffith, "Winning with Allies: The Strategic Value of the Afghan Model," International Security 30, no. 3 (2005): 124-160; Richard B. Andres, "The Afghan Model in Northern Iraq," Journal of Strategic Studies 29, no. 3 (2006): 395-422.

13 Amanda J. Snyder, The Politics of Piracy: Pirates, Privateers, and the Government of Elizabeth I, 1558-1588 (Wilmington: University of North Carolina, 2006).

14 CSIS and MacAfee, "Net Losses: Estimating the Global Cost of Cybercrime Economic impact of cybercrime II." Internet, http://csis.org/files/attachments/140609_rp_economic_impact_cybercrime_report.pdf (date accessed: 29 June 2014).

15 If the US IP Commission is current and IP theft costs the United States 2.2 million jobs per year, this alone accounts for the bulk of the US economic slowdown in recent years. July 2013 Testimony of former U.S. Senator Slade Gorton(R-WA), Member, The Commission on the Theft of American Intellectual Property (IP Commission) Before the House Energy & Commerce Committee; Subcommittee on Oversight and Investigations.

16 For a selection of representative arguments from Chinese officials see Danny Yadron and James Areddy, "China Hacking Is Deep and Diverse, Experts Say Intruders Often Work As Hackers For Hire, According to Officials," Wall Street Journal, 29 May 2014.

17 Richard B. Andres, "Cyber-Gang Warfare: State Sponsored Militias are Coming to a Server Near You." Foreign Policy (Feb 11, 2013). http://www.foreignpolicy.com/articles/2013/02/11/cyber_gang_warfare.

18 Hillary Clinton, "Secretary of State," Remarks on Internet Freedom from US Department of State, Washington, D.C., 21 January 2010. For an overview of US actions see Fergus Hason, "Internet Freedom: The Role of the U.S. State Department," Internet, http://www.brookings.edu/research/reports/2012/10/25-ediplomacy-hanson-internet-freedom (accessed: 29 June 2014).

19 See for instance, "Internet Freedom." U.S. Department of State, Internet, http://www.state.gov/e/eb/cip/netfreedom/index.htm (accessed: 29 June 2014). One of the more successful methods involves the U.S. Navy developing and disseminating Tor anonymizing software. See Liat Clark, "Don't trust privacy apps, use Tor," Wired UK, 14 June 2014).

20 The literature on the subject is large and growing rapidly. For representative work see Richard Lindsey, "What the Arab Spring Tells Us About the Future of Social Media in Revolutionary Movements," Small Wars Journal (July 2013); Stephen

NOTES

Metz, "The Internet, New Media, and the Evolution of Insurgency," Parameters (August 2012): 80-90; Jay Newton-Small, "Hillary's Little Startup: How the U.S. Is Using Technology to Aid Syria's Rebels," TIME, 13 June 2012.

21 Russian President Vladimir Putin regularly blames the United States for civil violence. See for instance: Moscow Times, "Putin Warns Against Letting West Use Anti-Kremlin Groups," March 7, 2014.

22 Clapper, James R. Statement for the record on the worldwide threat assessment of the US intelligence community, Senate Select Committee on Intelligence. Washington, D.C.: Office of the Director of National Intelligence, 2014.

23 See, Panetta, Leon E. "Remarks by Secretary Panetta on Cybersecurity to the Business Executives for National Security,." Speech, News Transcript from Secretary of Defense, New York, October 11, 2012.

24 For an analysis and survey of attacks see CSIS and McAfee. In the Dark: Crucial Industries Confront Cyberattacks. Washington, DC: Center for Strategic and International Studies, 2013. Makey, Edward, and Henry Waxman. Electric Grid Vulnerability: Industry Responses Reveal Security Gaps. Washington: A report written by the staff of Congressmen Edward J. Markey (D-MA) and Henry A. Waxman (D-CA), 2013.

25 A multi-year interagency study at the Institute for National Strategic Studies, National Defense University, examined how such an attack would translate into civilian deaths. It concluded that a worst case scenario would result in massive loss of life.

26 For work on potential scenarios leading to use of this type of capability see Goldamn, Emily, and John Arquilla. Cyber Analogies. Monterey, California: Naval Postgraduate School, 2014.

27 CSIS and McAfee. In the Dark: Crucial Industries Confront Cyberattacks. Washington, DC: Center for Strategic and International Studies, 2013.

28 Note that the more sophisticated SCADA malware often is not resident on a system but has accesses such that it can be moved onto the system when it is needed.

29 On a possible accidental use of a cyber-weapon against an electric grid see Harris, Shane. "China's Cyber-Militia." National Journal. (May 31, 2008) http://www.nationaljournal.com/magazine/china-s-cyber-militia-20080531.

Cyber Deterrence Isn't MAD; It's Mosaic

Ben Buchanan

Deterrence is always associated most strongly with Mutually Assured Destruction and nuclear weapons. Nevertheless, the fading memory of the Cold War should not leave a monolithic concept of deterrence as its legacy. In facing new threats and new actors, governments must develop a more nuanced and multi-faceted understanding of deterrence. Perhaps in no case is this more apt than threats in cyberspace. This article contends that there is no single way to deter an adversary's cyber operations. Rather, different actors and even different acts are subject to varying kinds of deterrence. Therefore, states must build a multi-faceted strategy to approach the cyber domain.

The argument consists of three steps. First, drawing on notions of deterrence that exist outside the Cold War, including in counterterrorism and law enforcement contexts, this article introduces the two main ways in which deterrence can vary: how much a threat must be deterred, which is correlated inexactly with its severity, and whether a specific actor is to be deterred or a large group. Second, it then places each variable onto a spectrum along an axis to construct a two dimensional model of types of deterrence. Different threats in cyberspace fit into different parts of

Ben Buchanan is a PhD student focusing on cybersecurity and national strategy at King's College London, where he is a Marshall Scholar. He graduated from Georgetown University in 2011 and received his Masters from Georgetown in Security Studies in 2013. He is a certified computer forensic analyst.

the model depending on their characteristics. Lastly, it describes how these forms of deterrence can together form the basis of a mosaic strategy for achieving realistic deterrence in cyberspace—and for recognizing where deterrence is not fully possible.

Before proceeding, it is worth clarifying an important definition: cyber deterrence is the art of deterring an adversary's cyber operations. It should *not* imply that a state's own cyber capabilities must be used in this effort. Indeed, a key part of the argument presented here is that the decision to launch a particular cyber operation can be predicated on factors that are entirely removed from cyberspace, including other military goals, the political context, potential consequences for individual actors, and more. Tools in these other areas thus can contribute to effective cyber deterrence.

Different Types of Deterrence.

Deterrence—the art of making another actor decide not to do something because of the threat of reprisal—is a concept that predates even the idea of statehood. As such, it is best to examine it in ways not bound to modern international relations. Drawing on work on deterring crime and political violence, Thomas Rid, amongst others, argues that there are two main theoretical distinctions between different types of deterrence. These two distinctions are particularly useful in their application to cyberspace.[1]

First, deterrence can be specific or it can be general. Deterrence against a specific threat involves crafting a set of punishments designed to respond to a specific action by a specific actor. Presumably, these consequences are tailored to cause meaningful pain to the actor.[2] General deterrence, in contrast, is the crafting of a set of punishments that are not targeted to any individual actor, but which could apply to any individual from a large and broadly-defined group of actors, should he or she perform an undesirable action. General deterrence often involves making an example of those who act in objectionable ways for others to see.

Second, deterrence can be absolute or restrictive. Absolute deterrence seeks to prevent any deviant behavior of a particularly damaging sort, such as the launch of nuclear weapons. Restrictive deterrence seeks to encourage other actors to moderate their behavior in either quantity or quality in order to reduce the likelihood of consequences. A simplistic understanding of deterrence rejects this distinction between restrictive deterrence and absolute deterrence. It states that every transgression should be deterred fully, and, if committed, punished massively. While attractive in its simplicity, such a model is not credible or effective.[3] Is a state really willing to use kinetic weapons to punish a relatively minor transgression like espionage against a mid-tier target? It is also undesirable because it poses escalatory risks. If a state is going to disproportionately retaliate against a relatively minor offense, it should not expect its retaliation to go unanswered. As a general rule, then, actors more often want to absolutely deter severe threats and are more credible when they communicate this desire. There is at least one exception: they might wish to deter actions that in themselves are not especially harmful, but could either provide the basis for greater destabilization or set a dangerous precedent.

In this two dimensional model, the United States' Cold War deterrence strategy that is so familiar to modern international relations the-

Applying the Model to Cyber Operations.

The two theoretical distinctions—specific versus general and absolute versus restrictive—can be plotted on two axes to form a two dimensional model, as below. Note that the most restrictive, but not absolute, point occurs just as the y-axis values turn negative; the lowest values of the y-axis are for activities where restrictive deterrence minimally applies.

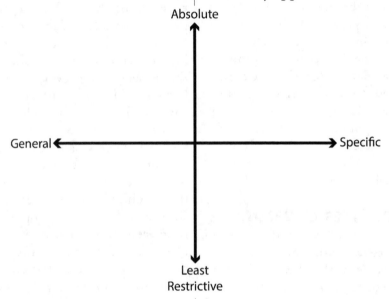

ory is in fact just one type of deterrence against one type of threat: absolute deterrence against the specific Soviet nuclear threat. This type of absolute and specific deterrence is alive and well today, given the nuclear deterrent many nations possess. It has only narrow utility, however, when applied to cyber operations. A more nuanced approach is required because many different threats exist in the cyber domain.

For any given class of threats, such as those posed by cyber operations, an actor can create a model to visualize what it seeks to deter. Some threats might be discrete points on the chart—where the actor and threat are known—while others are best represented as boxes, with heights and widths that reflect variability either in the specificity of the actor or the severity of the threat. Given the uncertainty of cyber operations, most will fall into this class.

For example, a model for the

United States might look something like what is below.[4] To be clear, this version is for purely illustrative purposes based on public domain information. Actual threat analysis would incorporate classified information and could well come to different conclusions. This model does not currently include a provision for assessing the relative likelihood of each threat, as threats either meet a threshold for inclusion or are left out entirely. To show some indication of relative likelihood, boxes and points can be given varying degrees of opacity. Limited discussion of each box follows below.

that cause widespread blackouts to the power grid, disable critical military systems like the Global Positioning System, or otherwise have significant or lethal physical consequences. China is often theorized as an actor with the sophistication to perform such an attack, and some speculate that its activities have been aimed at refining this capability.[7]

Russian Strategic Computer Network Attack: A Russian computer network attack might be similar to above in terms of its severity, but Russia is a different actor with a different set of calculations. In addition, the

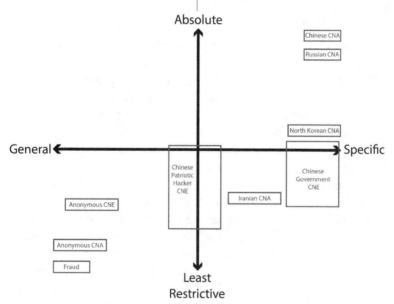

Chinese Strategic Computer Network Attack: There is no shortage of writers and strategists warning of the dangers of a strategic computer network attack, though skeptics question the likelihood.[5,6] Certainly, though, the damage of such an attack, if it were possible, could be immense. Activities in this category include attacks

Russians might choose an entirely different target. For example, they might be more inclined to target the American financial system, since they trade significantly less with the United States.[8] Thus, from an American perspective, what deters the Chinese might not deter the Russians, and vice versa.

North Korean Strategic Computer Network Attack: In theory, a strategic network attack need not come from an adversary with a heavy reliance on computers. Though it is unlikely North Korean computer network attack capabilities could match the Chinese or Russians in their lethality, the state has shown some willingness to use computer network attacks in the past, primarily against South Korea.[9] Since North Korea has relatively few cyber assets of its own to serve as the targets of American retaliation, and is internationally ostracized, the United States will again have to consider deterrence differently.

Iranian Operational Computer Network Attack: According to reports, the Iranians conducted the Shamoon attack against an American ally, as well as other direct attacks against American financial companies.[10] The available reporting suggests the attacks against U.S. firms were less severe than the Shamoon operation. It remains unclear if the Iranians' failure to truly impact the American financial system was due to a lack of capability or the effects of restrictive deterrence.

Chinese Computer Network Exploitation: While the dangers of Chinese network exploitation are widely reported, they are unquestionably less immediate than the imagined devastating strategic computer network attacks.[11] They therefore receive less of an absolute deterrent. This box refers to the best hackers directly associated and under the control of the Chinese intelligence and military services. They thus may be open to certain models of deterrence aimed at Chinese decision-makers.

Chinese Patriotic Hackers Computer Network Exploitation: There are reports of a number of hacking groups acting in concert with general Chinese interests without direct affiliations with the Chinese government.[12] In their exploitation of American (and other) networks, these groups are not primary under the control of the Chinese decision-makers, but may in some ways be protected by them. They have their own capabilities, which can be assumed to be less than those of the best Chinese military and intelligence units, and their own incentives. They thus are deterred differently, and may be more suited to a general rather than specific approach.

Anonymous Computer Network Exploitation and Attack: The independent hacking group Anonymous, along with offshoots such as LulzSec, has demonstrated a willingness to hack American government entities, financial providers, and universities.[13] Their computer network attacks are reasonably unsophisticated—mostly minor denial of service attacks—although some of their exploitation operations have been effective, such as those against Stratfor and HB Gary.[14] Given that they are an ad-hoc collective, they are primarily subject to general deterrence.

Financial Fraud by computer criminals: There are a large number of mostly faceless computer criminals who make money through identity fraud, so-called ransomware, and surreptitious Bitcoin mining. They frequently target Americans. While they can pose an economic nuisance and can be deeply detrimental to individuals, they are not of primary concern to American national security policymakers.

The Mosaic of Cyber Deterrence—and Its Limits.

Every deterrence strategy begins with attribution. Without it, the entire discussion is moot. Since attribution is a complex problem worthy of its own detailed discussion, this paper accepts the assertion of American policymakers that the United States can perform attribution when targeted with a cyber operation. Certainly, recent American rhetoric and actions has been designed to draw attention to its attribution capabilities, with an eye to creating foundations for deterrence. Prominent examples of this are former Secretary of Defense Leon Panetta's bold claim that, "Potential aggressors should be aware that the United States has the capacity to locate them and to hold them accountable for their actions..." and the indictment of five Chinese hackers believed to be affiliated with the Chinese People's Liberation Army.[15, 16]

Even when a state's attribution capabilities are known, there is no single dominant strategy that meets each cyber challenge. Rather, the United States should construct a mosaic of different deterrence strategies to confront the full spectrum of cyber threats. The differences in these assorted types of deterrence loosely correspond to the four quadrants of the model. Even so, cyber deterrence alone is incomplete. Policymakers must advance defensive measures as well.

Strategic computer network attack, spanning the top two quadrants, can be deterred in two ways. It can first be deterred with the threat of a retaliatory computer network attack, in the same way second strike capabilities were positioned during the Cold War. This relies on the existence of realistic and sufficiently important targets to strike with a cyber attack.

If no such targets exist, the United States can employ the second method of deterrence: kinetic equivalency. This doctrine states that the attacked state will deploy its conventional kinetic arsenal to retaliate for a cyber attack. It is particularly useful for deterring states that do not have many cyber targets, like North Korea, or that could, in extreme circumstances, potentially disconnect themselves from the internet, like China. The United States has already made such a declaration of equivalency.[17] Whether it is viewed credibly is hard to know, as no state has yet tested it. Other states without the overwhelming power-projecting capabilities of the American military might find this doctrine hard to promulgate credibly.

Since kinetic retaliation is not a credible threat in response to every infraction, states must develop alternative pieces of the deterrence mosaic. Operational cyber attacks by a specific enemy that are not strategic in their outcome, such as the Iranian attack against the American financial system in 2012, fall in the bottom right quadrant. They are intrusion. Indeed, most intrusions go undetected for months, if not years, a challenge to the foundation of attribution on which deterrence is based.[18] Second, states suffering exploitation are unlikely to be the

Since kinetic retaliation is not a credible threat in response to every infraction, states must develop alternative pieces of the deterrence mosaic.

therefore subject to more restrictive deterrence. According to the mosaic model, an adversary who launched this kind of attack should suffer some consequences, but not as severe consequences as one that launched a strategic attack. Examples of such mid-tier punishments include diplomatic protest, isolation from internet governance bodies, and black-holing of internet traffic from a targeted range of IP addresses. Policymakers have the option of clearly spelling out their "red lines"—essentially, what is in the top right quadrant and what is in the bottom right—or of leaving them deliberately ambiguous, with the hope of deterring a broader range of activity than they are actually willing to punish.

Deterring exploitation by states and those who are their direct agents is much harder (this group is also mostly in the bottom right quadrant, with some small overlap into the top right). First, exploiters may feel they are less likely to suffer deterrence because there is no immediate damage to alert the adversary of an

first to launch an attack in response. Nevertheless, some forms of deterrence can be theorized.

For actors directly linked to the state, such as sophisticated foreign intelligence agencies, it may be possible to communicate, potentially in secret, some gradations of severity. Doing so can provide some narrow absolute deterrence and a greater deal of restrictive deterrence. For example, any exploitation or attack that potentially might harm America's nuclear umbrella could prompt a fiercer response than economic espionage. In this way, then, even sophisticated foreign entities directly linked to the government could be directed away from the most serious targets. Deterring their activities against less critical, but still deeply important, targets is much more difficult. Some restrictive deterrence is still possible, such as sanctions or indictments if economic espionage crosses a certain level.

In the case of hackers loosely affiliated with an adversary's government (who, because they are sometimes known and sometimes unknown, mostly span the bottom two quadrants), some combination of narrow absolute deterrence and restrictive deterrence is necessary, but not sufficient. These hackers, absent formal government protection, must be careful not to go too far, lest the targeted country retaliate against them and their host government decline to protect them. As a result, they are likely to avoid some targets entirely and employ the utmost discretion when hitting others. There are limits to this restrictive deterrence, however, and limits to how well absolute deterrence can be communicated when the threat is more general. Such deterrence is based in large part on the hacking group's collective and self-reinforcing perceptions. It is unlikely to be effective through the framework of traditional criminology. Here, the goal of the state should be to achieve maximum deterrence while recognizing that it can never truly eliminate the threat. The state should focus on identifying the truly capable hackers who pose a legitimate threat and apply restrictive deterrence to them, discouraging them from high value targets. In the short history of these hacking groups, these sophisticated hackers have thus far focused on exploitation against mid-tier targets, which may reflect their ideology, capability, or successful restrictive deterrence. Because it is difficult to identify in advance who poses a threat, the state should employ techniques from general deterrence used in traditional criminology. It should

Thoughtful use of positive incentives...may better contrast the punishments and encourage hackers to be economically productive for the state rather than a thorn in its side.

in stopping them from exploiting mid-tier targets, since the hackers are presumably protected enough by their government to withstand any response, minimal as they believe it is likely to be.

In the above model of cyber threats facing the United States, two sets of hackers not even loosely affiliated with a state comprise threats in the bottom left quadrant. Hackers not associated with any state but instead motivated by political intention, like Anonymous, are best viewed use the punishments it delivers to some hackers as a warning to others, taking care to be proportional in these punishments. There is one key difference between these hackers and other criminals: while theft and murder have little social value, those with computer skills can be useful to the state. Thoughtful use of positive incentives—some of which may be political in nature, such as minor concessions on political grievances—may better contrast the punishments and encourage hackers to be economically productive for the state rather than a thorn in its side.

Hackers not associated with any state and motivated by money, such as identity thieves, are nearly impossible to absolutely deter. When such hackers are overseas, their own governments may have willful ignorance of their activities. In the long run, this group should be approached with traditional restrictive deterrence. This probably means attempting to set up agreements of international cooperation to make it more difficult to escape punishment. In the short run, where prosecution is possible it should be pursued, but the United States will likely have to recognize the limits of its power to deter in this regard.

Conclusion: The Limits of Deterrence.

There are significant limits to even the best mosaic of cyber deterrence. Given the amount of computer fraud, state-sponsored exploitation, potentially-state-sponsored exploitation, and hacking collective activity against the United States, restrictive deterrence is at best a necessary but insufficient solution. Absolute deterrence thus far seems to fare better, but it is difficult to prove a negative, especially while the possibility of strategic computer network attack is subject to such debate. A final conclusion, then, is that the mosaic must be accompanied by strong cybersecurity practice. This includes, but is not limited to, careful network monitoring, patching, and penetration testing.

These defensive countermeasures should have two main goals. First is keeping general adversaries, such as Anonymous, from being able to conduct strategic attacks. Absolute deterrence may not be as effective against them, because there is little of value to retaliate against, because attribution is particularly difficult, or because they simply might not care about the consequences of retaliation. Second is minimizing the

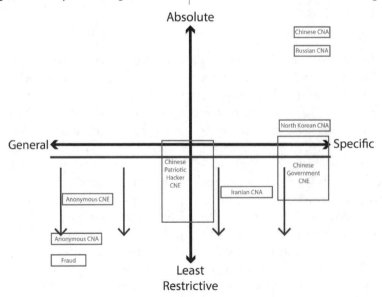

harm that adversaries who are only subject to restrictive deterrence, such as patriotic exploiters in China or operational attackers in Iran, can do. The figure below summarizes the barrier and downward pressure these defensive measures are designed to create.

This focus on defensive measures alongside deterrence is a break from the traditional understanding of deterrence in international relations. Historically, in situations that call primarily for absolute and specific deterrence—such as the Cold War—excessive defensive measures can be destabilizing because they hamper an adversary's ability to perform a second strike. In that case, preserving stability was more important than defense and so anti-ballistic missiles were mutually banned. In the case of cyber deterrence, as in criminology, defense is not destabilizing. There are two main reasons for this. First, further escalation—to kinetic weaponry—is always possible, so the fear of a devastating first cyber strike that renders a powerful state like the United States or China unable to respond does not apply. Second, it is easy, and obviously correct, to justify any defensive cyber measures as a means of supplementing restrictive deterrence. Such countermeasures are widely accepted and broadly recommended—though certainly not always implemented fully—so their presence is not questioned. Defenses, coupled with a smart mosaic of deterrence, are therefore a key part of keeping cyberspace safe.

The author would like to thank Professor Thomas Rid of King's College London for reading an earlier draft of this article.

NOTES

1 Rid, T. "Deterrence Beyond the State. The Israeli Experience." *Contemporary Security Policy*, April, vol 33, iss 1, p. 124-147. 2012. DOI:10.1080/13523260.2 012.659593

2 In some constructions specific deterrence can require actually enacting the punishment. In international relations, however, where the punishments are likely to have grave and broad consequences, this seems unreasonable. Instead, specific deterrence in international relations relies on credible communication of consequences to the deterred actor, which requires knowing specifically who the actor is.

3 Shavell, Steven. "A Note on Marginal Deterrence." *International Review of Law and Economics*. 1992. 12, 345-355.

4 A similar model could be constructed by the Chinese or Russians regarding American activity in cyberspace. The American model is presented here because, based on public reporting, it appears the United States faces a broad range of threats, while the Chinese and Russians are likely targeted most prominently by the United States' National Security Agency. Further, there is simply more public reporting on the range of threats facing the United States.

5 "Remarks by Secretary Panetta on Cybersecurity to the Business Executives for National Security, New York City." Department of Defense. http://www.defense.gov/transcripts/transcript. aspx?transcriptid=5136 Panetta's Cyber Pearl Harbor speech.

6 Rid, Thomas. Cyber War Will Not Take Place. 2013. Oxford University Press.

7 Capaccio, Tony and Bliss, Jeff. "Chinese Military Suspected in Hacker Attacks on U.S. Satellites." *Businessweek*. 27 October 2011. http://www.businessweek.com/news/2011-10-27/chinese-military-suspected-in-hacker-attacks-on-u-s-satellites.html

8 "U.S. Trade in Goods by Country." US Census Bureau. https://www.census.gov/foreign-trade/balance/

9 "North Korea 'behind cyber attack' on South websites." *BBC News*. 10 July 2013. http://www.bbc.co.uk/news/world-asia-23324172

10 Perlroth, Nicole. "In Cyberattack on Saudi Firm, U.S. Sees Iran Firing Back." *New York Times*. 23 October, 2012. http://www.nytimes.com/2012/10/24/business/global/cyberattack-on-saudi-oil-firm-disquiets-us.html?pagewanted=all. Gorman, Siobhan and Barnes, Julian. "Iran Blamed for Cyberattacks." *The Wall Street Journal*. 12 October 2012. http://online.wsj.com/news/articles/SB10000872396390444657804578052931555576700

11 Clarke, Richard. "How China Steals Our Secrets." *New York Times*. 2 April 2012. http://www.nytimes.com/2012/04/03/opinion/how-china-steals-our-secrets.html. See also "APT1." Mandiant. 18 February 2013. http://intelreport.mandiant.com/Mandiant_APT1_Report.pdf

12 For one example, see Markoff, John. "Vast Spy System Loots Computers in 103 Countries". *New York Times*. 28 March 2009. http://www.nytimes.com/2009/03/29/technology/29spy.html

13 Wakefield, Jane. "Anonymous Wikileaks supporters explain web attacks." *BBC News*. 10 December 2010. http://www.bbc.co.uk/news/technology-11971259. Kao, Joanna and Solomon, Ethan. "Anonymous Hacks MIT." The Tech. 15 January 2013. http://tech.mit.edu/V132/N61/anonymous.html. Sheets, Connor. "NSA Website Down Following Apparent DDoS Attack Possibly By Anonymous Or A Foreign Government." International Business Times. 25 October 2013. http://www.ibtimes.com/nsa-website-down-following-apparent-ddos-attack-possibly-anonymous-or-foreign-government-1442452

14 Anderson, Nate. "Anonymous vs. HBGary: the aftermath." *Ars Technica*. 25 February 2011. http://arstechnica.com/tech-policy/2011/02/anonymous-vs-hbgary-the-aftermath/. Meyers, Michelle. "Report Details Extent of Anonymous Hack of Stratfor." CNET. 27 December 2011. http://www.cnet.com/news/report-details-extent-of-anonymous-hack-on-stratfor/

15 "Remarks by Secretary Panetta on Cybersecurity to the Business Executives for National Security, New York City." Department of Defense. http://www.defense.gov/transcripts/transcript. aspx?transcriptid=5136 Panetta's Cyber Pearl Harbor speech.

16 Schmidt, Michael and Sanger, David. "5 in China Army Face U.S. Charges of Cyberattacks." *New York Times*. 19 May 2014. http://www.nytimes.com/2014/05/20/us/us-to-charge-chinese-workers-with-cyberspying.html?_r=0

17 Gorman, Siobhan and Barnes, Julian. "Cyber Combat: Act of War." *Wall Street Journal*. 31 March 2011. http://online.wsj.com/news/articles/SB10001424052702304563104576355623135782718

18 The median number of days until detection is 243. "Mandiant Releases Annual Threat Report on Advanced Targeted Attacks." *Mandiant*. 13 March 2013. https://www.mandiant.com/media-room/release/mandiant-releases-annual-threat-report-on-advanced-targeted-attacks1/

Managing Asymmetries in Chinese and American Cyber Power

Greg Austin

The need for cyber détente between the United States and China in cyber space is spelled out in a 2012 policy paper by the EastWest Institute (EWI).[1] It argued that both countries want some reduction in tension over military and political activities in cyberspace, and called out the asymmetry of power between the two countries in cyberspace as an important aggravating factor in the relationship. The paper advocated clarification of military strategic concepts of information dominance and preemption. At the Munich Security Conference in February 2013, an EWI briefing went further. It identified an urgent need at the global level to shape new understandings of strategic stability in cyber space by arguing that powerful states were driving for the technological frontier in military cyber capabilities, but paying little attention to the impact of such a push on the insecurities of their potential enemies or rivals. The briefing argued for "an explicit commitment by states to strategic stability in cyberspace within the framework of a fully articulated foreign policy and national security doctrine." In light of the sustained attention to China's recent cyber espionage inside the U.S. government and in the public domain, this short article expands on one question central

Greg Austin is a Professorial Fellow at the EastWest Institute, focusing on cyberspace and defense policy. He previously served as Vice President for the Worldwide Security Initiative, and is an author and editor of five books on China, including his most recent work, *Cyber Policy in China*.

to the problem: How does China view the United States' drive for dominance in cyber military power? This article argues that China views this as a threat to its security in a fundamental and game-changing way that undermines the possibility of a shared vision of stability in broader geopolitical relations. Many in the United States feel much the same way about China's emerging cyber power, though with less justification, given China's backwardness relative to the United States.

This article draws a sharp picture of China's "cyber" security dilemma. While there are useful analyses of where cyber military capability sits in China's strategic vision, most only briefly touch on China's sense of insecurity in the military cyber domain and how the fear of United States' cyber superiority could be driving China's plans.[2] This article takes the view that even as China may have closed the gap in some conventional military armaments between it and the United States, the gap in cyber warfare capability has

depth of modern digital information and communications systems and technical expertise available to their adversaries."[3] Ball, who has worked for more than two decades researching the signals and intelligence capabilities of both the United States and China, has assessed that "China is condemned to inferiority in IW [information warfare] capabilities for probably several decades."

U.S. Cyber Dominance. China is
now the biggest manufacturer of desktop computers, and recently claimed the position of building the fastest supercomputers in the world. There are other indicators of China's increasing capability in cyberspace, not least its espionage and its domestic surveillance. But Americans' invention and U.S. corporations' global commercialization of the internet, coupled with U.S. economic power and unchallenged preeminent position in advanced science, information and communications technology guaranteed its position as the single most powerful country in

The United States and its allies exchange sensitive cyber technologies with each other in ways that not only exclude others, but in ways that are intended to maintain cyber superiority in as many domains as possible...

probably widened. While we need much more information to reach a confident assessment, on the basis of available evidence, this author is inclined to agree with Desmond Ball's assessment that China's military leaders must be in a state of "despair at the breadth and

terms of wealth and power generated from the cyber domain. Beyond its pre-eminence in the civilian sector, the United States has a military strategy premised on "information dominance." It has been leading the world in developing information dominance as a military strategy, with associated weaponry, dedicated units, and dedicated planning elements in the Pentagon: the uniformed services and the intelligence agencies.

The United States sees itself as "preeminent in the fields of Intelligence, Cyber Warfare, Command and Control, Electronic Warfare and Battle & Knowledge Management," in the words of the Deputy Chief of Naval Operations for Information Dominance.[4] This military cyber power has combined with the country's pre-eminent conventional and nuclear forces, its superior economic power (twice the annual GDP of the nearest competitor), its global supremacy in the ICT industry, and its unequalled scientific capability to entrench in global affairs the "unipolar moment," a term coined in 1990.[5] This meant then, as now, that the United States is the lone superpower in world affairs.

This position is reinforced by the alliance relationships that the United States has established. In his very first observation about this unipolarity, the concentration of geopolitical gravity in the United States, Krauthammer included the Western alliances as a primary foundation of that power.[6] At that time, these included NATO members, Japan and Australia. Since then NATO has expanded, at the same time as countries like South Korea and Saudi Arabia, both members of the G20, have become solid allies of the United States on global issues beyond their own regional concerns. NATO is now actively cooperating on cyber defense with around ten countries outside its 28-member state alliance. This expansion of the American alliance

base is central to understanding the political economy of the cyber world in the second decade of the 21st century and how China sees it. The largest flows of finance, investment, trade, and technology are still amongst the United States and its allies. This historically unprecedented suite of alliances entrenches the strategic power of the United States in the cyber realm relative to all countries outside that alliance. The United States and its allies exchange sensitive cyber technologies with each other in ways that not only exclude others, but in ways that are intended to maintain cyber superiority in as many domains as possible, whether it be military, technological, or commercial.

Countries outside the alliance include China, Russia, Brazil and India. The degree of exclusion from the alliance system varies for each of these. India has recognized the power of this alliance and is campaigning to be seen as a "like-minded country." It has secured the support of key Americans to be brought into the fold as an ally in cyber policy. For China, the picture is very different. From the point of view of many in the United States, China (like Russia) is definitely a "cyber adversary." This case is made in a number of places. One of the most prominent has been the 2011 report of the National Counter-Intelligence Executive.[7] The report observed that China and Russia see themselves as "strategic competitors with the United States," and "are the most aggressive collectors of U.S. economic information and technology," relying heavily on "open source information, human intelligence (HUMINT), signals intelligence

(SIGINT), and cyber operations—to include computer network intrusions and exploitation of insider access to corporate and proprietary networks." Their purpose, the report suggests, is to advance their own "national security and economic prosperity" by gaining a "competitive edge over the United States and other rivals."[8] In his 2013 State of the Union address on February 12, President Obama used the term "our enemies" without naming China only two days after leaked reports of

nology and powerful armed forces to weaken or deter other states remains a primary goal. Yet for five centuries, the idea of strategic stability has proven to be a useful illusion. It sustained the idea that states can craft a sense of mutual satisfaction with geopolitical realities and contain the urge to further militarize and heighten military confrontations. The concept was always more political, and comparisons of military capabilities between rival countries was only ever one part. In fact, the idea of

China is concerned not just that the United States may have better cyber warfighting capabilities than China does, but that it can be used creatively as part of the total force package for strategic effects in other areas of war-fighting, the economy, and politics.

a new National Intelligence Estimate singled out China as the most serious threat to the United States in cyber space.

In the cyber world, China—weak in cyber military power—has no cyber capable allies, except maybe Russia.[9] The United States—stronger in cyber military power than any other country—has at least twenty.[10]

How Good is China's Military Cyber Capability relative to the United States? Strategic stability as a public good may be an illusion in situations where the most powerful states can be divided into groups which contest fundamental political doctrines and values, and where development and deployment of advanced military tech-

stability was not so much intended to contain improvement of capabilities as it was to shape military competition to make it more predictable, transparent, and to link it to political goals. The most serious manifestation of strategic instability in 2014 between the United States and China is the absence of mutual satisfaction with geopolitical realities in cyberspace and the concern that new cyber military capabilities may have undermined previous tendencies toward tension reduction by altering pre-existing assumptions of military power.

In this regard, it is important to understand that China (like the United States) does not see cyber military power as a question of computer versus computer, network versus network, or hacker versus hacker. China sees cyber military power as the leveraged relationship between military cyber assets and other forms of military power. This approach is described well in the following definition of 'cyber conflict': "broader than cyber warfare, including all conflicts and coercion between nations and groups for strategic purposes utilizing cyberspace where software, computers, and networks are both the means and the targets."[11]

Yet even if one limits the assessment of relative cyber military power just to China and the United States, it is plain not just that the United States is well ahead, as discussed below, but that it has used this to change the leveraged relationship between military cyber assets and other forms of military (and political) power.

In understanding this, we should not be distracted or overly preoccupied by China's cyber espionage. According to U.S. public and private sources, China appears to have scored some big successes in cyber espionage. By comparison, it is unknown how good the Americans have been. The Chinese successes suggest that the United States' defenses against some espionage are quite weak. Yet espionage is only a small fraction of the total picture of cyber military power.

How do we understand Chinese and American relative capabilities and the sense of insecurity created by the leveraged application of cyber military assets for strategic stability? There is not a detailed, public domain assessment of U.S. cyber military power, let alone a net assessment relative to China, leaving aside the impact of cyber assets on U.S. strategic planning in areas like

nuclear strikes. In discussing the question with former U.S. senior military officers, the following determinants of United States military cyber power were judged to be essential reference points for understanding, and also to be seriously lacking in China's case:

• A strong tradition of joint operations refined in combat operations around the globe, almost non-stop since the Goldwater Nichols Act of 1986, but taking hold in the second half of the 1990's.

• Long experience of direct application of cyber operations in combat, beginning most notably in 1999 against Yugoslavia.

• An advanced private sector, with appropriate incentive mechanisms, to provide contractor services in military applications of IT.

• Access for unilateral purposes to a large talent pool of government technical staff, intelligence and university-based researchers from across its global alliances.

• The human and technical intelligence collection capabilities needed for effective cyber offensive operations against military targets.[12]

China's 2010 National Defense White Paper demonstrates how good China thinks its information warfare capability is. Addressing only the first point above, it notes that China has obtained only a "preliminary level" of interoperability between different elements of its armed forces within this sphere.[13] If China is weaker in joint operations, then it is weaker in cyber war capability. The corollary of that statement is that China sees itself as weak in joint operations, and so it sees its failure in military cyber power relative the United States. Some of the best informed American sources with knowledge of China's capabilities have concurred with this broad-brush assessment in discussions with me. China's armed forces are well short of their military cyber goals relative to the United States.[14]

China also sees itself as weaker and more dependent on the United States for development of the civilian cyber sector, which underpins the country's military cyber power. China definitely sees itself as lagging well behind in civil technology and protection of civil assets from U.S. cyber attacks. It knows how difficult it is for a country to achieve a level of technological preparedness in its armed forces that is significantly different from the technological foundations of the society as a whole (talent base, R&D climate, investment levels). A number of Chinese and international studies have consistently ranked China fairly low in terms of advanced cyber information technology.[15]

One element that needs to be factored into an assessment of Chinese perceptions of its relative capability in cyberspace is its sense of vulnerability to cyber-enhanced attacks. China is concerned not just that the United States may have better cyber warfighting capabilities than China does, but that it can be used creatively as part of the total force package for strategic effects in other areas of war-fighting, the economy, and politics. As much as the United States has been concerned about Chinese cyber intrusions into U.S. critical infrastructure, China shares similar concerns. Its government and its researchers have moved much more slowly that the United States in

addressing cyber threats to its critical infrastructure.

As with the issue of cyber espionage being something of a distraction from the core issue of relative cyber military power in Chinese eyes, the prominence accorded by Western observers to Chinese attacks on civil infrastructure is also not the core issue. Such attacks are a threat and would affect military capability, but China (like the United States) does not see civil infrastructure as the main game in cyber warfare or in assessments of relative cyber military power. For China, the main focus is capability in all aspects of the military domain, referred to by Americans as C4ISTAR (command, control, communications, computers, intelligence, surveillance, target acquisition, reconnaissance). China focuses on assessing and defending against U.S. capabilities to degrade China's C4ISTAR in three fields: strategic nuclear operations, theatre missile operations against Taiwan or Japan, and conventional operations.

China is seriously planning for cyber warfare operations against the United States, and possibly more so than it is preparing for naval or air combat operations. China's cyber warfare capability is probably far more powerful but less lethal than its conventional military capabilities. That suits China enormously in both respects. China's military strategy is highly defensive, but to defend against possible U.S. operations against it over Taiwan, China has to rely mainly on unconventional operations, and these include cyber operations as well as psy-ops of the classic kind. In November 2012, China announced it would speed up the informatization of its armed forces, a term that includes both military operational cyber dimensions as well as more basic computerization of the military. In February 2014, China announced it would do everything necessary to become a cyber power. In June 2014, China officially established a Cyberspace Strategic Intelligence Research Center in its General Armaments Department.[16]

What to Do? "Strategic Cyber Stability" Talks.
The reduction of military tension between China and the United States and the establishment of some mutual predictability in their military planning is an agreed aim of both countries.[17] The negative impact on this goal of the asymmetry of

(land, sea or air) as long as the total number of warheads was equivalent and key strategic concerns of the other side were addressed. However, states do not have any agreed understanding of strategic equivalence or strategic stability in the cyber age. There is little understanding of how strategic stability might be achieved between adversary pairs so visibly separated by a large, military cyber asymmetry.

As foreshadowed by Joseph Nye and Bill Owens in 1996,[18] there is not even wide acceptance of a fundamental reality that cyber warfare capabilities affect strategic nuclear warning time, classic notions of deterrence, and second strike capability. Fortunately, there is a private view in some senior U.S.

China is seriously planning for cyber warfare operations against the United States, and possibly more so than it is preparing for naval or air combat operations.

power between the United States and China has not been comprehensively analyzed. Above all, there is a structural dilemma. States expect negotiations to result in reciprocal obligations, and in many cases these are unconsciously conceived as being equal or symmetrical in some way. For example, arms control agreements between the USSR and the United States were premised on strategic equivalence in which each side would adjust its forces in different ways judged to produce an overall, mutually acceptable outcome. The two sides accepted differences in numbers of particular strategic nuclear systems

military circles that the United States should abandon pre-emptive (first strike) aspects of its cyber war doctrines, and move to a doctrine of strategic stability in cyberspace. In cyberspace, such a doctrine may be the closest we can get to the doctrine of strategic parity, which in the Cold War was one of the primary concepts underpinning the reduction of the risks of nuclear war.

A landmark 2011 study from the Carnegie-Tsinghua Center for Global Policy on China's reactions to the most recent U.S. nuclear posture review canvassed the new importance placed by China's leaders on the concept of strategic stability.[19] The report advocated the opening of dialogue with China on what strategic stability between it and the United States might mean. While the report noted that Chinese sources see this as the main characteristic of the military relationship between the United States and China, there is no direct mention of the impact of cyber weapons on Chinese or American views of their relationship.

The United States does appear to have a choice: maintain its doctrine of information dominance and cyber pre-emption, thereby threatening many of the diplomatic gains in U.S.-China relations of the last 15 years, or begin talking to China about what a new posture of "mutual" security in cyber space would like. The task will be massively difficult, given the high sensitivity of the issues and the highly compartmentalized character of expertise on cyber warfare issues as they affect strategic stability. This engagement would not be about counting missiles that can be photographed from space or making technical assessments of missile range and readiness levels. This would be about finding confidence-building measures at a political level that can accommodate the complexities not just of cyber warfare, but also of the broader China-U.S. strategic relationship. The linkage made by senior U.S. officials between China's cyber espionage and the entire fabric of U.S. economic and industrial competitiveness imposes an even bigger burden on that relationship than that imposed by linking a country's human rights policies and American preparedness to conduct normal diplomatic relations. The cyber asymmetry is causing some-

thing akin to a cosmic disturbance in bilateral diplomacy, for which officials on both sides have few responses. While cybersecurity might be one of a long list of bilateral issues, a case could be made that it has morphed into an over-arching fundamental reality in the past decade. The core diplomatic challenge of the bilateral relationship is how to manage persistent asymmetries in cyber military power between China and the United States because it so fundamentally affects the main security interest of both sides.

Several commentators have observed that China's massive use of cyber espionage against foreign cyber assets, civil infrastructure, and military technologies may be related to its relative weakness. One point often not canvassed is the incentives that China would need to see on the table for it to even consider some abatement of its current activities. The even tougher question is what would abatement look like in an environment where China's rivals are not showing any interest in curtailing their own espionage, and there is interest in maintaining doctrines of pre-emptive cyber-strike and "information superiority." In March 2014, U.S. Defense Secretary Chuck Hagel, said in remarks at the National Security Agency that "outside of government networks," the United States would exercise restraint in cyber space, and was urging other states to do the same.[20] But this does not address the cyber power asymmetries between China and the United States.

The 2013 U.S.-China working group on cyber security, now suspended after recent U.S. indictments of five Chinese uniformed personnel for industrial espionage, was a useful start. Yet the working group came after a decade of confrontation in cyber space, and probably incorporates the wrong people to address the two countries' asymmetries of cyber power. The 2012 agreement between Russia and the United States that added a cyber warning component in their bilateral nuclear risk reduction center is a useful precedent, but its value is weakened in the China case because of the approximate parity of the nuclear arsenals of both sides. The U.S.-Russia agreement is premised on recognition of the direct link between cyber war capability and strategic nuclear stability. Similarly, to make progress in the U.S.-China case, both sides need to recognize that the military cyber domain is not independent or a discrete component of military power. Cyber power has redefined military power, and China is very weak. How can the United States ease this security dilemma for China? How can China come to accept that its actions, though defensible in many ways, discourage the United States from cooperative behavior on military aspects of cyberspace?

There is only one answer. Both countries have to agree on a shared concept of sufficiency of defense in cyber space; they have to agree on how cyber capability affects strategic nuclear capability and conventional force readiness; and they have to commit to measures of mutual restraint in civil and military uses of cyberspace. That is a huge and protracted agenda. But in the absence of this vision as the end point, any bilateral cyber dialogue, including by well-meaning NGOs and research institutes, will be fruitless. Refusal to commit to such a vision by both sides or by just one of them—which means acceptance of the belief that strategic superiority is achievable and meaningful for nuclear-armed countries—would negate 40 or 50 years of progress in security thinking, and may undermine everything that we achieved in our understanding of strategic self-sufficiency and mutual security.

Continuing reliance on expectations of reciprocity and of equivalence may be not only misplaced but a threat to peace. This may be more relevant to the strategic approach of China than that of the United States, but heavy reliance by either state on an assumption of strategic equivalence of cyber military power and a demand for a resulting policy reciprocity will become a serious threat to mutual security. For Chinese leaders, the cyber military capability of the United States, attended by its dozens of cyber allies, has irreversibly and fundamentally transformed pre-existing assumptions of strategic stability and China's security, because this has enhanced the United States' global military and economic pre-eminence.

Disclaimer: This article represents the views of the author and not necessarily those of the EastWest Institute.

NOTES

1 Austin and Gady, "Cyber Détente between the United States and China: Shaping the Agenda".

2 See for example, Magnus Hjortda, "China's Use of Cyber Warfare: Espionage Meets Strategic Deterrence", Journal of Strategic Security, Volume IV, Issue 2, 2011, pp. 1-24. Annual reports by the United States Department of Defense to Congress on military developments in China offer useful and balanced comments on some aspects of China's military cyber capability but do not address China's sense of cyber insecurity as a dominating reality of its military planning. For some treatment of this issue, see Greg Austin, Cyber Policy in China, Polity, 2014 (forthcoming), chapter five.

3 Desmond Ball, "China's Cyber Warfare Capabilities", Security Challenges, Vol. 7, No. 2 (Winter 2011), pp. 81-103, p. 101.

4 "The U.S. Navy's Vision for Information Dominance", May 2010, p.1, http://www.insaonline.org/assets/files/NavyInformationDominanceVision-May2010.pdf.

5 This phrase was coined by Charles Krauthammer, "The Unipolar Moment", Foreign Affairs, Vol. 70, No. 1, America and the World (1990/1991), pp. 23-33.

6 He wrote: "The center of world power is the unchallenged superpower, the United States, attended by its Western Allies" (p. 23).

7 United States. Office of the National Counter Intelligence Executive, "Foreign Spies Stealing U.S. Economic Secrets in Cyberspace: Report to Congress on Foreign Economic Collection and Industrial Espionage 2009-2011", October 2011, http://www.ncix.gov/publications/reports/fecie_all/Foreign_Economic_Collection_2011.pdf.

8 Ibid. p. 4.

9 A senior Russian official told me that Russia views China as less trustworthy in cyberspace than the United States.

10 This point needs considerable analysis beyond the scope of this paper since the way alliances play out in cyberspace is very different from traditional patterns. At one very simple level for example, sharing of information with allies is much less common than it is for conventional military capabilities and plans.

11 Healy 2010 but replayed in the authoritative CSSA report "Addressing Instability in cyberspace", 2010.

12 For arguments on similar themes, see the briefing by Oxford Analytica, "China Will Speed Up Military Cyber Development", November 14, 2012.

13 "A preliminary level has been achieved in interoperability among command and control systems, combat forces, and support systems, making order transmission, intelligence distribution, command and guidance more efficient and rapid. Strategic planning, leadership and management of informa-

tionization have been strengthened, and relevant laws, regulations, standards, policies and systems further improved. A range of measures, such as assembly training and long-distance education, have been taken to disseminate knowledge on information and skills in applying it. Notable achievements have been made in the training of commanding officers for joint operations, management personnel for informationization, personnel specialized in information technology, and personnel for the operation and maintenance of new equipment. The complement of new-mode and high-caliber military personnel who can meet the needs of informationization has been steadily enlarged."

14 One diagnostic indicator cited by two sources was United States' superiority in space-based assets, which they regarded as absolutely central to effective cyber operations at the strategic level of war.

15 This was the conclusion of a 2011 study by the Chinese Academy of Sciences, Information Science and Technology in China: A Roadmap to 2050. The study also registered broad agreement, though in visible disappointment, with a set of IT competitiveness rankings by The Economist that placed China 50th in global terms, out of 66 countries surveyed. See Li Guojie (ed.), Information Science and Technology in China: A Roadmap to 2050, Chinese Academy of Social Sciences, Science Press, Beijing, Springer, 2011, pp. 20-21. A similar view can be found in the World Economic Forum's 2014 Network Readiness Index (NRI), which had China sitting at 61st in world rankings for its use of information technologies to advance its national competitiveness and its citizens' lives. China had slipped from 36th in the 2011 rankings. The NRI gives only a partial picture of China in cyber world but it mirrors quite critical sentiment within the country about its weak position relative to others. The United States, Japan, Singapore, Taiwan, South Korea and Malaysia are all ahead of China in the 2014 NRI. See World Economic Forum, The Global Information Technology Report 2014, April 2014, http://www.weforum.org/reports/global-information-technology-report-2014. See also Austin, Cyber Policy in China, chapter four.

16 Chinamil.com, "PLA Cyberspace Strategic Intelligence Research Center founded", 30 June 2014. http://eng.chinamil.com.cn/news-channels/china-military-news/2014-06/30/content_6025789.htm

17 There are sound reasons for this originating in policy and academic analysis. On the scholarly side, as outlined so aptly by Jack Snyder and Barry Posen in their 1984 books, The Ideology of the Offensive and The Sources of Military Doctrine, a state with offensive doctrines, and an institutional disposition to offense, is more likely to miscalculate in favor of a decision for war than states with defensive postures and an institutional disposition to defense.

AUSTIN **Military Matters**

NOTES

18 As observed in a famous 1996 article in Foreign Affairs by Professor Joe Nye and Admiral William Owens, "The information technologies driving
America's emerging military capabilities may change
classic deterrence theory." Joseph F. Nye Jr and
William A. Owens, "America's Information Edge",
Foreign Affairs, 1996 (March/April), http://www.
foreignaffairs.com/articles/51840/joseph-s-nye-jr-
and-william-a-owens/americas-information-edge.

19 Lora Saalman, "China and the U.S. Nuclear

Posture Review", Carnegie-Tshinghua Center, Carn-
egie Endowment for International Peace, Beijing,
Feb 2011, See http://carnegieendowment.org/files/
china_posture_review.pdf/.

20 Jim Michaels, "Hagel encourages 'restraint' in
cyber warfare", USA Today, 28 March 2914, http://
www.defensenews.com/article/20140328/C4ISR-
NET07/303280032/Hagel-encourages-restraint-
cyber-warfare.

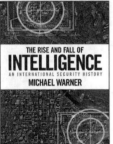
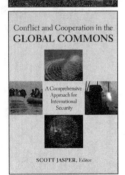

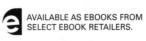

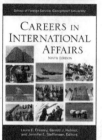